MADGE

Coloured Memories

Andrew A. Karalius

AuthorHouse™ *UK Ltd.*
500 Avebury Boulevard
Central Milton Keynes, MK9 2BE
www.authorhouse.co.uk
Phone: 08001974150

: This book is a work of fiction. People, places, events, and situations are the product of the author's imagination. Any resemblance to actual persons, living or dead, or historical events, is purely coincidental.

© 2010. Andrew A. Karalius. All rights reserved

No part of this book may be reproduced, stored in a retrieval system, or transmitted by any means without the written permission of the author.

First published by AuthorHouse   11/10/2010

ISBN: 978-1-4520-3612-0

This book is printed on acid-free paper.

FOREWORD.

Whilst writing this book I was worried about using the correct punctuation. My computer kept urging me to use hyphens and semi-colons. When I'm reading a book, the overuse of the above annoy me. I decided to write how I like to read… simple. Commas. Full stops, question marks and the occasional hyphen.

I never set out to change the world when I started writing this book. It's just a book! So, if you're looking for a few hours of entertainment, this maybe for you.

If you are looking for a Shakespearian masterpiece, put this book down. I like to use basic English language… and not a semi-colon in sight!

ACKNOWLEDGEMENTS;

There are lots of people who have touched upon my life. Some of whom have had a big influence on me.

I would like to thank all those people who have helped me along the way. My sister Donna, who has been the one ever-present in my life. Gill Gaughan and Paul Turnbull for believing in me and for their financial backing. Ian Potter for his kind words of encouragement.

Mr.Kirwan and Mr.Yeats, the only two teachers who inspired me enough to go to school. I'm sure when you went into teaching, if you could change just one kids life, that would have been enough. You did… Mine. (Eventually) Thank you.

Gerard Dolan (cover photography).

My family for enduring endless hours of keyboard tapping and temper tantrums when things weren't going right.

I'd also like to thank all the people in this book who are no longer with us… you are all fondly missed.

Authorhouse publishers for their support and patience with a first time Author. My wonderful wife Louise, without whom I would never have wrote this book. You truly are 'The wind beneath my wings.'

Finally I would like to thank my five beautiful grandchildren. Lily-Marie, Honey, Annie, Charlie and Oliver… just for being here!

Thank-you, one and all.

Oh… and I'd like to mention Matty Milburn, because he paid me ten-pounds to do so.

INTRODUCTION;

After the death of my mother, my life spiralled out of control. Loss, self-pity, anger, self-destruction, alcohol and many panic attacks later. I eventually ended up in Walton Prison in Liverpool. It was there I decided to write my story.

I would write the days events on every scrap piece of paper I could get my hands on, not a diary. Scribbles I would eventually try and put together after my release.

The first thing I had to do was sit my bum in the chair, that's where the hard work really begins. I sat looking at a blank computer screen for over half an hour. Where do I start? I decided if I was going to do this I should tell the story of why I ended up in prison, my life leading up to that point.

Why? Many people asked, what is so extraordinary about your life, why would people want to read about your childhood?

Maybe they won't but I'll give it a go anyway. I went back as far as my memory would take me, the beginning. That's always a good place to start…

In Loving Memory of Madge... My Mum.

Marjorie Mary Holland, born New Years Day 1935, at Whiston Hospital. An unspectacular person, except to me. She was my mum, though to most people she was simply known as... Madge!

It's only now at Forty years of age that I can start to understand what Madge had to endure during her relitavely short life. She was just fifty six years young when she died of lung cancer and although the world didn't change on that day. Mine certainly did.

CHAPTER ONE

WHEN WAGON WHEELS WERE BIG!

My first memory of home was living at 26 Sinclair Avenue, with my Gran, sister Donna who is seven years my senior and of course Madge. It was a quiet area littered with the sort of characters any writer could only dream of. I say quiet, this was with the exception of match days as our house was located directly across from Naughton park, the home to Widnes rugby league club. Every other Sunday it would be chaotic, it did have it's advantages because every time a goal kick was taken the ball would inevitably go over the perimeter wall and into our waiting arms. I must have collected dozens of size five Mitre rugby balls over the years.

The best thing about the location of our house was that if a game was being televised you could see the gable end of the house which had a window. One of my mates would go upstairs, open the window and pull a moonie. All we could see down stairs on the television was a small arse sticking out of our landing window in the background, no matter how many times we did this the comedy value never seemed to diminish. Even now at my age I still find it hilarious.

Sinclair Avenue was only a stones throw away from the town centre although you wouldn't know it living there. Every garden had a huge Elm tree, until the summer of '73 when ninety per cent of them were wiped out by Dutch Elm disease and had to be chopped down. This was probably a godsend to most car owners as the sap and bird poo would play havoc with the body work of their new off the line Vauxhall Vivas' or Ford Cortinas'. Very much the car of the day but to us kids it was a catastrophe as they provided hours of entertainment for they were challenging but every bit climbable.

We did have a playing field, it was just in front of our house and next to the Rugby ground, it was nicknamed the half moon because of it's shape. I was a small boy with mousey blonde hair, I had a huge Cows Lick in the middle of my fringe, it caused me problems way into my Teens. I also had a speech impediment, due to a large gap in my two front teeth. I'm not painting a very good picture of myself, I know. I couldn't pronounce my L's. My sister, Donna would sit me down and say;

'Lips... Lemons... Legs.' Emphasing the L.

'Now you say it.' She'd say.

'Wips... Wemons... Wegs.' Was my response. It drove her mad. Even when I finally mastered the the use of the letter L, I would pretend not to... just to annoy her.

The house was my gran's and we were there as a result of Madge's turbulant divorce from my Dad. I was just a baby when all this occurred so don't remember any of it. My sister was almost nine and I think it had a profound effect on her. To this day I think it's probably shaped the person she has become, don't get me wrong she's not turned out too bad but like most of us, she has her own issues.

She was Daddy's little girl for seven years until I arrived, she even got to pick my name. This was because Madge was told by Doctors that the sex of her first child would determine the sex of any subseqent children. Donna was expecting a baby sister and definately not a boy. When she was told the baby factory had run out of baby girls and would have to have a baby boy instead she was distraught, inconsolable I believe. Many expensive presents later and negotiations to rival that of the Northern Ireland peace talks she reluctantly let me join the family. There was one last proviso and that was she could pick my name. She decided on Andrew, When later asked why she'd picked that particular name she said it was in honour of Andrew Gardner. (A news reader of the day.)

'Why him?' Dad asked.

'Cos I hate him.' Was her reply.

Not a good start then. Our relationship didn't get any better as we grew older, probably due to the seven year age gap and the fact that I definately wasn't Mikaela Amanda. The name I was given when they thought I was going to be a girl, she however was still daddy's little girl and I was a proper little mummy's boy. Madge wrapped me up in cotton wool. I seem to remember being quite happy back then. We had a good solid foundation, my mum, sister and my Gran, who was the Matriarch of the family and kept everyone in check. We also had my Aunty Fiona, Madge's

Madge

older sister who lived across the road with Uncle Paul, she was a big stern woman and had the same attributes as my gran, she was also the Aunty who had money. Madge had two more sisters, Pat who was the youngest and rarely showed her face and then there was Bella, her and Madge were like two peas in a pod and she was always at grans' house. There was my Aunt Kit just down the road, who incidentally wasn't my real aunty, in fact I'm not quite sure if she was any relation at all but in those days if someone bought you a birthday present or watched your house while you were out that was enough ... they're practically family and you had to address them as such. Any one it seemed over the age of consent must be addressed as Mr or Mrs and certainly not by their first names.

This was the seventies and showing your elders respect was paramount, there was Mrs Harrison, an old spinster who lived next door to Aunty Fiona, to this day I never got to know her first name. Madge would send us to Mrs Harrison to get loose cigarettes until she got paid, this wasn't just her lending people fags she actually sold them and if you borrowed seven off her you would have to give her ten back on pay day. Fuck me! It has only just hit me as I sit here writing ... old Mrs Harrison was a dealer, she'd probably get arrested these days. She was small and hunched over with long greying hair and old national health glasses. She'd look at you over the top of them. 'Do you have a note from your mam?' She'd growl. Despite the fact Madge would be stood at the front door about forty yards away across the road waving in acknowledgment that it was safe to make the transaction of seven Woodbines. Mrs Harrison had a strict code of conduct and she wouldn't compromise, no note, no merchandise and you couldn't plead to her better nature, she didn't have one. Apart from that she had a dog named Timmy, it was as old as she was with brown and black matted fair with tints of grey but he was twice as nasty, you couldn't walk past the gate without it running at you growling and yapping. Despite living there for several years I don't remember any of them ever dying, I bet the two of them are still alive with a combined age of three hundred and two, only now they've probably dealing in sim cards or nicotine patches.

Then there were Mr and Mrs Mackeral and their son Ste whom acquired the original nickname of 'Fish.' Mrs Mackeral was one of the younger generation of neighbours, still ancient in our eyes of course but one step further away from having to drink her tea from a beaker than the other neighbours. We even got away with calling her by her first name, Ivy. Which made her without doubt the coolest mum on the street, though to be fair, Madge was quite cool and hated being called Mrs Karalius, particulary given the fact that after the divorce she reverted back to her maiden name 'Holland.'

Donna and I kept our Dad's name, mainly to avoid any confusion at school and in any case Donna was old enough to decide she still wanted to see Dad at the weekends. I however decided not to. I suppose so as not to hurt Madge .

The oddest neighbour we had was probably Sarah, a close friend of Gran's. She insisted that we called her by her first name. Well she would, her second name was Shizeaple, her father fled Austria before the first World War and settled in the area. But when translated into English it read 'Shitapple.' It's just as well she never had kids, that would have been cruel. She lived on the opposite corner to us, she was about seventy or so with a big bulbous red nose and always wore a headscarf. She stood about eight feet tall, alright I'm exaggerating but she was tall. Especially for a woman in those days. To say she'd let her garden grow was an understatement, it was like a jungle and provided my mates and I with no end of fun. Finally next door were two sisters Bessie and Dolly, about the same age as Sarah, in complete contrast they were about four feet tall and they walked sideways, due to some chemical imbalance in their ears that afflicted them during their later years. I don't ever recall hearing any of them speak, and their nickname, yes youv'e got it... The crab sisters. Kids can be cruel.

My favourite memories of the early years at Sinclair Avenue was the house itself. It was always busy, somebody would always be there drinking tea out of gran's best china, putting the world to rights. My cousins always running in and out, Sarah visiting at least ten times a day. I guess the saying is true, you really could leave your door open in those days. Aunty Fiona was the most frequent visitor. She always seemed to have an ailment, inspiring Madge to rename her 'Vera Vallium.' Though she never knew this and had she, it would have caused much offence.

On one occasion however, had she not been there complaining I may not be here writing about her complaining. I think it's not to melodramatic to say she probably saved my life. I was only about Four years of age and don't recall much of the event but I can relay them to you in all confidence the details are accurate because they went down in family history and were retold several times over the years each time becoming more remarkable. I had a bad tooth infection and it made me quite poorly. I developed a high temperature and had a convulsion making me swallow my tongue. While everyone was panicking not knowing what to do Aunty Fiona apparently calmly walked into the kitchen, got a spoon, put it down my throat and retreived my tongue and then carried me over to a neighbour who also happened to be an Ambulance man.

Although I don't recall much of this I do recall the consequences of it. The Doctor gave Madge a bottle of green medicine which helped to bring down my temperature. I viewed this as a miracle cure and my life jacket and if I couldn't physically see that bottle of green medicine stood on the pantry shelf I would go into a state of panic. I never actually used it again but for years it stood pride of place on the top shelf, just in case. Looking back I think it was nothing but a placebo, a clever bit of child pshychology on Madge's part .

The whole episode turned me into somewhat of a hypocondriac, to this day I still am I suppose. If I have a headache it's a tumour. Indigestion ... heart attack and I still rely on my green medicine, although they now take the form of 'Migralieve.' I occasionally suffer with migraines and no matter where I am, if I don't have them on my person the panic sets in. Back then I think it's fair to say it would get to ridiculous proportions. I recall one day eating a blade of grass, then making Madge eat one as well. On another occasion I licked one of my toy soldiers and made Madge do the same. I suppose my train of thought, being a child, was that if anything happened to me that Madge would come with me. There was also the time when I ate cat poo, yes, Madge had to eat some as well, or at least she said she did. I noticed things were getting smaller, I once asked Madge why Wagon Wheels, my favourite snack were getting smaller;

'They're not son, your hands are getting bigger.' She replied.

I panicked, was the fact that my hands were getting bigger normal. For some weeks after I was comparing hand sizes with kids my age.

I have to feel sorry for Mr Robinson, the ambulance driver whom I afore mentioned. The amount of times he must have seen me getting carried down his path by a family member with one ailment or another. Usually self inflicted it must be said. Like the time I was trying to pull a loose tooth out with an elastic band and inadvertantly shot it down my own throat. Or the time I swallowed an ice cube and was choking on it, by the time Donna carried me over to Mr Robinson it had melted . The look on his face told a thousand stories. I'm sure every one of them consisted of me and my family leaving him alone, to be fair to him, he was quite new to the area and we didn't even know him that well. He and his family moved on after only a relatively short time in Sinclair Avenue ... for the life of me I can't think why.

I do recall one occasion that wasn't self inflicted. Madge liked playing

Bingo and frequented the local Bingo hall several times a week and usually dragged me with her. These weren't like the Bingo halls you get today. This was the type where you put tokens in and when your numbers were called, you would slide over a plastic cover to hide your number. They were usually accompanied by an arcade of some description. Of course that was something I could live with, I mean playing arcade games or going to school, no contest. One of the prizes on offer for a full house was a massive plastic safari park, perfect size for my soldiers. I'd been mithering Madge for weeks to get it for me if she won but she always reminded me that I got enough. On this particular day whilst playing space Invaders, I started to get a slight pain in my stomach. I informed Madge but given my reputation for hysterionics she told me to stop and give me ten pence for another game. The pain got worse until I was doubled up on the floor of the arcade screaming in agony. A crowd gathered and Madge ran over in sheer panic, partly because she didn't beleive me at first and partly because she only needed two fat ladies for a diagonal. The Safari was brought down off the wall.

'Look son, I've bought it for you … your Safari.' It was good but not a miracle cure for a possible burst appendix.

I was rushed up to the doctor's, in a taxi no less. What happened next was hilarious to all the family except Madge. I remember sitting in a packed doctors' waiting room doubled over in agony, then all of a sudden the pain just dissapeared but was replaced by the most horrendous smell. It appeared I'd been suffering with trapped wind which was now very much untrapped. Madge was mortified, not only had she had to forfeit her possible 'diaganol.' She'd also spent a small fortune on a Safari for my soldiers and a taxi to the doctor's. Only to be completely embarrassed in front of the whole waiting room by the smell that I'd just released from my bum. You would have thought Madge would've been pleased at me not having a burst appendix and I'm sure she was but she hid it well, as all I recall is being dragged out of the Doctor's surgery by the scruff of the neck, Safari in tow with the words 'You little Bastard' ringing in my ears.

1974 was a bad year and the beginning of the end of 26 Sinclair Avenue that we knew and loved. This was the year my Gran Holland died, ironically of Lung cancer. Madge always said she'd hate to die that way, with family sat around the hospital bed waiting for her to take her last breath and hooked up to an endless amount of wires and machines. My most vivid memory of my Gran dying was not seeing my first dead person or indeed the funeral.

Madge

I was six years of age and remember sitting in the living room at number 26 with Donna and Madge. This was her's and Aunty Bella's night off from keeping vigil at Grans' bedside at Clatterbridge Hospital in Liverpool. Aunty Fiona and Aunty Pat would take this watch. We sat there watching 'Petrocelli` at about 11.15 at night, the last thing on television on that particular night. We heard an almighty bang. When I say bang it was as if somebody had picked up an old tin dustbin and dragged it over the roof of the house. It was a weird sound. Madge and Donna just looked at each other, then at me. It was just a noise as far as I was concerned but to them it was a sign and not a good one. Within minutes there was a knock on the door. We all looked at each other again, finally Donna got up to answer it.

'Mum, it's Mrs Harrison.' She said.

I remember thinking 'I hope she's not brought Timmy.' She hadn't but she'd brought something far worse, the news of my Grans' death. Mrs Harrison and Aunty Fiona were only two of the few who had a telephone in those days, it seemed fitting that she should be the one to bring the bad tidings on that fateful night. Along with Sarah she was one of Grans' oldest neighbours. She even brought Madge seven Woodbines ... until payday of course. I looked at Madge and remember her expression, it was like her whole world had just crumbled, for fucks sake it probably did. She immediately hugged Donna and I.

Grans' death devastated Madge, that was obvious but the only good that came from it was the reintroduction of my dad. Upon hearing of Gran's death he seized the opportunity to come back in Madge's life, much to my relief. She needed somebody to help her through and although he wasn't ideal, he was there. This was the first time in my life that I realised how money can wreck a family. My gran never left a will and it was widely assumed that she had left her money somewhere inside number 26. With this my Aunties ascended on the house and looked in every nook and cranny to no avail, nothing was ever found. They left the house in a mess, I just remember Madge sat there crying, I just couldn't believe why my usually solid family were acting like they were on a supermarket sweep and continuously reminded Madge this was not her house and they could do what they wanted. To be fair, it was their mum as well. I just thought they could have been a little bit more sensitive.

After their fruitless search they still weren't satisfied, they then started dividing all of Gran's belongings and furniture between them. It must be said Aunty Bella had very little involvment in this, she was more concerned how this was affecting Madge, Donna and myself. She only took a couple of memento's, the house was now a shadow of it's former self. We were left with the basics or should I say everything nobody else wanted. Madge was only four foot eleven and three-quarters, she always stressed the 'three-quarters' as it made her nearly five foot and of slender build, she could be feisty and I was surprised she didn't put up a fight, looking back now I don't think she cared. She'd just lost her mum and her best friend.

Madge had an unlikely ally, my dad. When he saw what had occured, he, along with uncle Vin completely redecorated the house to a modern standard and added some smart furniture and ornaments. The house was now beginning to feel like her own and it soon would be, as she had been living there for some considerable time with gran, the council let her continue the occupancy in her own right. A fact not yet known to Aunty Fiona, not until one Sunday afternoon when she walked in, arms folded as usual and with a look of disdain regarding the new interior.

'Mam wouldn't approve of this.' She said before proceeding up the stairs.

'Where are you going?' Asked Madge. Before Fiona could come up with the now predictable one liner of 'This is my mam's house.' Madge produced the all important rental agreement ... in her name.

'Now get out of my house.' She said in a calm but stern manner. They never spoke for a while afterwards and I think Madge regained back some self respect on that day.

At first the new regime at number 26 appeared to be going fine. Madge and my Dad were on speaking terms for the first time in years, (sort of) there was no chance of us becoming your average two point four child family. That boat had well and truly sailed but it was amicable.

Dad would come and do jobs for Madge and in return he would get some dinner and even a pleasentary now and then. They would sometimes sit up until two in the morning relating to Donna and I stories of their youth. The time when they met The Beatles, or the time when my dad as a boy tried to poison my grandad Holland's horse he used whilst working as a milkman. I think this is where my interest in writing came from. I was fascinated by the stories relating to real life. I could almost picture myself there with them, the problem with these tales are credability because no matter how much you recall a situation you will only ever see it from your perspective and it becomes very difficult to be objective. Nevertheless, I found it very easy to accept these stories on face value, why not ? Who's it harming if the truth had been distorted a little, besides, I loved it and for the first time in my short life, Madge and my dad seemed normal, even Donna was being nice.

My idea of eutopia was not to last for much longer. Dad would stay away for days on end working, it was those days the deterioration of Madge seemed to start. When dad wasn't there Sarah would come over and keep Madge company. Sarah loved her Whisky and they would sit there indulging in a tipple whilst reminiscing about my gran Holland. There didn't seem any harm in this at first but it became more frequent, particulary in the absence of my dad, it became clear that Madge was slowly slumping into a state of depression.

What happened next would be forever etched on my memory, dad had installed a telephone in the house and it seems ironic that had he never, things may have been so different. I don't recall Madge actually receiving this particular phone call but I do remember her telling Donna and I to get ready as we were going out. She phoned a Taxi and off we went, we ended up in Halewood in Liverpool.

Upon arrival a child of about fourteen came running out to greet us, she was in tears and handed Madge some money to pay the Taxi fayre. I recall Donna asking Madge what was going on and why were we here, Madge just ushered us in this strange house and up the stairs. On top of the stairs sat another young girl also in tears, she was about my age, still puzzled, Donna asked the young girl her name and what was going on. Before the girl could give any sort of response we heard a key open the front door, we all stopped and looked over the banister to see who it was. The door opened and there stood my dad, so this is where he'd been. Madge opened the living room door and stood face to face with him, the young girl lept up and shouted 'Daddy`...WHAT! Dad's face went white, I've never seen him speechless before, or after come to think of it. Donna it seems got her wish after all, a sister, albeit not quite the way she planned it.

It turns out the phone call was from the Daughter of the woman my dad had been seeing for years and the main reason for the divorce. She somehow got our number from dads' belongings and when her Mum, who was an alcoholic incidentally, took an overdose, she thought she'd get hold of my dad on this number. Instead she got Madge, Madge in turn ran to this woman's aid, phoned an Ambulance and looked after the children until Social services arrived. What was never expected was dad turning up.

Dad was very much ostracised again and Madge's drinking became more and more erratic. It didn't help that Aunty Bella got her a job in the local Labour club as a barmaid, a renowned hot spot for late night boozing.

When I look back at my life in Sinclair Avenue during the years after gran Holland died. I just see dark winter nights and a time I associate with the colour grey. Yes, I longed for the days before gran died. When Summer seemed to last forever. When laughter was ever present, when it always snowed at Christmas... and when wagon wheels were big!

CHAPTER TWO

THE LABOUR YEARS.

By the time I was eight years old, Donna had spent more time looking after me in the past year or so than Madge did. Instead of working the initial one night a week at the Labour club Madge would spend as much time there as she could, probably to escape the house. We never really saw the benefits of her working as she would spend most of her money on the frequent stay behinds that the club was renowned for. It was normal for her to come home as late as four in the morning and never in a good state. The only bit of hope Donna and I could cling to was that she would be so drunk she would just sleep it off, if she was just drunk enough to stand, that's when all hell broke loose. Donna usually got the brunt of it, I think because she still visited Dad and Madge saw this as fraternising with the enemy.

By this time the drinking was taking its toll and Madge was letting the house go downhill. The once modern interior which Dad had done was now shabby and unkempt, she even sold all the expensive ornaments Dad had bought to neighbours and family members. The leather padded doors were now off their hinges, probably due to the constant slamming and just stood against the open doorway.

When Madge had that one whisky too many her eyes would change, they would become glazed and manic looking. When this happened it was time to get out of the way, Donna named this 'Madge eyes syndrome.'

Sarah often accompanied Madge on such nights, she would claim it was to make sure she got home safely but I think it was so Sarah could indulge in yet more after hours drinking. I recall her always having a bottle of Scotch under her arm, she was almost Eighty but could probably drink most young men under the table.

On one such night Sarah came into the house before Madge and walked into the living room carefully moving the leather door to one side but foolishly replacing it once she was inside the living room. I say foolishly because Madge was not far behind her and in her drunken state forgot about the door being unhinged, she pushed the door open but instead it fell and landed directly on top of Sarah.

'Where are you Sharah ... Sharah...' Madge drawled.

'I'm umder da fecking dower.' Replied Sarah. For some reason when she had one too many she'd become Irish.

Still bemused, Madge then stood on top of the door much to Sarah's discomfort and started to wobble because of the unsteadiness of Sarah's body underneath. She fell backwards and just lay there, everything went quiet. I shouted Donna out of bed, she came down the stairs, just looked at them both in disgust and assured me they were only drunk and told me to go to bed.

Donna slept like a baby that night, or probably not but she'd become hardened to this sort of thing and she had to. After all this was becoming a regular occurance.

I stayed on the settee and never got much sleep, when I did I remember being woke by a groaning noise. It was Sarah under the door, I got up and struggled to move the heavy door from on top of her, she just stood up straight and all one side of her face and hair was flat where she'd been lay for several hours. She still had hold of her bottle of scotch and never spilled a drop, she took one last swig, about turned, stepped over Madge then staggered across the road to her house.

I tried to wake Madge but she was well and truly out of it. I just covered her with a coat that was hanging on the banister and went back to the settee. I missed school again the next day and this became a habit, it's fair to say in the last ten years of my school life I must have missed over fifty per cent of it. Not just because of Madge, although her lack of enthuiasm to get me there didn't help.

I can look back now and recall some of those late night antics as hilarious, although at the time they were anything but.

On another occasion Madge had staggered in after yet another late night at the Labour club. This time shouting Donna down the stairs just to give her more abuse and hiding tablets down her bra pretending to have taken an overdose. Again Donna was wise to the attention seeking,

I however used to become hysterical. After Madge finally going to bed, I remember lying on the floor at the side of Donna's bed wrapped in my quilt. I often did this as I never felt safe on my own in that house after gran died, sometimes Donna would let me lie there and sometimes she'd tell me to get out of her room. On those occasions I'd sit on the small landing waiting for it to become light outside.

This particular night I remember Madge shouting that she had a 'Plane' in her head, she repeated it several times.

'She's pissed again.' Donna assured me.

But she repeated several times about having a 'Plane' in her head, Donna and I went into her room and sure enough she was lay there with the wing of a Lancaster bomber stuck out of the side of her head. She'd fell over in her drunken state and landed on one of my Airfix models, I don't know how I felt. I was scared for Madge as it looked quite deep but I was also annoyed because it took me hours to assemble the 'Lancaster bomber' that now lay in pieces.

The Labour club years weren't all bad, just those late nights that we used to dread, in fact when Madge wasn't at the club I used to love sitting up with her talking about her younger years and the things she and dad used to get up to. I could see in her eyes that those bygone years still provoked happy memories for her and for a few brief moments we were normal again. We would make toast on the bars of the old fireplace and it always tasted great, it was probably awful but I didn't care. I was with my mum and there was no whisky in sight.

I recall the summer of '79 five years after gran had died and although Madge was still drinking it was now mainly confined to the weekends. It was a glorious hot summer and the neighbours would organise fun days for the kids which consisted of athletic events on the half moon. I was eleven years old and after the six weeks holiday was about to embark on another chapter of my life in the form of secondary school, it was one of the best summers I can remember. There would be events nearly everyday, 'Ivy Mackeral' would give out trophies for the fastest kids to run around the half moon, although her son 'fish' would win most of them. I think that's probably why she organised it, he would be the one with the newest football kits, the best toys in the street and he'd constantly remind us of it.

I remember my first football kit, I say kit but it was more of a mix and match. I was a 'Manchester United' fan, Madge could not afford the kit so I ended up with a Norwich City top accompanied by a pair of Bolton Wanderers shorts but it was a kit of sorts and I felt like a white 'Pele.'

This was also the summer where society started going mad, the time when people started locking their doors. I recall Donna, who was now Eighteen coming home and telling Madge that a man had exposed himself to her, this was big news and almost unheard of. The police got involved and I don't know if they ever caught him or not but I do remember parents tightened security around us kids and would tell us not to talk to strangers and report to them anything out of the ordinary.

This was the first time I heard the word 'weirdo.' There were several reports of 'flashers' that summer, it must have been the heat but there were also warnings of men in cars watching young children playing. I didn't understand what the implications of this was and our parents were being very diplomatic in explaining what these men might do if we went off with them, we just knew it wasn't good.

Stories of such events even made the local news, we were made to watch, so we would get the message and if we saw any such men we should tell our parents straight away.

It was on a scorching sunny day that I had such an encounter. I was running down the wing on the half moon in my Norwich Wanderers kit with the ball at my feet, I took on 'Johno,' skipped inside 'Smiggy' and was about to put the ball in the bottom corner, this was it, my moment of glory, my last minute FA cup final winner then... BANG ! I was clattered to the ground, by 'Fish,' who else. As I stood up and looked around I saw a silver car parked outside Sarah's house. I could hardly make out what kind of car it was due to the heat of the newly tarmacked road obscuring it but I could see a man sat inside. I thought I recognised him but I couldn't think where from, despite all the warnings I waved in his direction. He just looked and smiled, he then turned his head and looked at our house for a moment then looked back at me, put his hand up as if to say 'bye' and drove off.

I later told Madge about the incident, she immediately picked me up by my hand, threw a coat over my head and ran with me over the road to Aunty Fiona's house. Looking back I don't think the U S President of the time enjoyed more security than I did that day. The police were called, they asked me questions about the car and the man inside, they also asked the other kids what they'd seen but they all said they saw nothing as they were to busy playing football. I got the feeling no one quite believed me but even now I know what I saw. I never saw that car or man again and never really thought about it much after.

Regardless of what happened that day, it's fair to say that the image of summer had been shattered. Everyone was more cautious now and wary of people they didn't know and they had to be as I remember, several news reports of around that time regarding children across the country being taken by strangers. It seemed to be an epidemic, a scurge of the times. The days when the words 'pervert' and 'weirdo' became part of everyday vocabulary.

This was also the summer I learnt a valuable lesson, never bend down under an opened paint tin ... Every summer the council would come around and paint the window frames and doors. On this particular day we were all playing in the garden. I bent down to tie my laces, my positioning was pinpoint as right above my head on the pantry windowsill stood an opened tin of white gloss. To be fair the painter had stood it on some putty so it wouldn't fall off but it was just my fucking luck that at precisely that moment the sun had melted the putty and the paint fell and covered my head. Panic set in, the sort of panic you momentarily get when you think you've got your head stuck in a fence. Donna thought it was hilarious, furiously I chased her around the half moon dripping with white gloss. It took weeks to get that paint out of my hair but years for the reliving of it, it became the stuff of legends.

The summer of '79 passed with plenty of incident but alas September came, it was time for me to start secondary school, although school was not top of my list of priorities I was quite looking forward to starting 'Wade Deacon High School.' Madge had saved to buy me a new uniform which consisted of a tie, blaser, white shirt and black trousers. I was paraded arounded neighbours and family members houses to show off how smart I looked. Madge told me how some years ago she'd been to a fortune teller and he told her her son would end up in uniform...

'He was right' she beamed.

Of course he was right, I remember thinking. All kids end up in uniform when they go to High school, I didn't tell her that, I didn't want to ruin the moment.

My first morning of 'Big school' arrived. Madge and Donna made sure I didn't forget anything and I remember them both waving me off that day, they looked proud, I however was shitting myself. The only thing that made me feel a bit better was my best mate, Mike Ericson seemed even more terrified than I was. After the initial trepidation it was fine and I enjoyed it, we made new friends and everything was good, for a while anyway.

My enthusiasm for school soon dwindled, after a year or so Mike and I started to play truant, it started with the odd day here and there but the more we got away with it the more frequent we'd do it. Madge had her own demons to deal with and didn't notice the fact that my home work was becoming less and less with each passing week.

Each morning we would get ready for school as normal only instead of having our school work in our bags, we would fill it with a change of clothes. Sarah's garden was a great foil, we would double back and hide in her garden for half an hour or so and get changed. Mike wore a bright pair of yellow canvas trousers and I wore a bright red pair, very much the fashion of the day. This particular day sticks out more than most, we'd decided to go to Widnes market where we would steal 'Star Wars' figures from the toy stall. Why we did this I don't know, we'd stole one each and decided to go back for more. This time the stall holder was aware of what we were up to and was waiting, after sliding the box down our tight conspicuously coloured trousers we headed for the exit. To our horror we heard the stall holder shouting and running after us, we ran but just as we got to the entrance he caught us, he clipped us both around the ears and took back the Star Wars figures. We got off lightly because he could have called the police and that would have blown everything.

I remember looking at Mike and he was crying, not because we'd been caught but because he'd pissed himself out of fright. I would normally find this hilarious if it wasn't for the fact that I also had pissed myself, we both stood there in our bright coloured pants with steam coming from them. As if that wasn't bad enough we had to walk a mile or so back to Sarah's garden so we could change back into our uniforms.

We never spoke about that day again and swore that we should never tell another soul what happened at Widnes market and to this day I never have, until now... Sorry Mike!

Our criminal days were over and it wouldn't be long before our truanting days were brought to an abrubt end. Upon returning home from a 'hard days schooling' I was confronted by Madge, Aunty Fiona and a truant officer. As I walked in the living room Aunty Fiona stood there and with arms folded she said;

'Where have you been?'

'School.' I replied with an air of arrogance.

With that she grabbed my bag off my shoulder and emptied the contents on the living room floor, of course there was no school work just my change of clothes. I was caught red handed and after a stern talking to by the truant officer it became clear I would have to start attending school or be put in the naughty boys home.

Madge never shouted at me over playing truant but I sensed the dissapointment in her, I'd let her down. She had enough on her already fragile plate without having this one added burden.

To be fair the Labour club had it's advantages, Madge started to work saturday afternoons and would take me along where I would be allowed to do some glass collecting, in return the old men would give me money on which I would spend playing pool. I had hours of fun and turned into quite a good player but that was the only good thing that came from that place. Ironically I ended up having my wedding reception there some years later, Madge had been dead for some time but I swear when we were doing the speeches I thought I caught a glimpse of her in the background standing behind the bar. Maybe that was just wishful thinking as I would have loved her to be there... Perhaps she was?

Donna was now at the age where she was going out with friends for a drink at the weekends and didn't have the burden of having to mind me while Madge was at the club working. A relief to Donna no doubt but not to Madge, I was only twelve and had to be minded and given the time she'd arrive home it would have to be a sleepover.

An arrangement had been made with Jean White, who lived at the end of Sinclair Avenue. I didn't mind this much as her son Tony was one of my mates and at least I didn't have to see Madge rolling in at four in the morning rotten drunk. I stayed there every Friday and Saturday for about two years and remember thinking what it would be like living in a normal family. As well as Tony there was his brother Gary and his sister Bev, then there was Ernie, their dad, he would always be doing things with his kids. Taking them on days out, playing football with them, a far cry from my dad who I'd not even seen for some time.

Every Saturday and Sunday morning I could never get in our house as Madge was in bed until at least two in the afternoon sleeping off the night before. This was even the case on Christmas morning, Christmas '82 to be exact. I recall looking through our window at my new bike in the living room but couldn't get it because Madge was dead to the world and wild horses wouldn't have woken her up. Christmas eve was a big night at the Labour club and she'd probably not got in until about four in the morning, so my Christmas would have to wait a bit longer until until she got up or Donna came home.

I finally got to ride on my 'Grifter' on Boxing day as by the time I got in the house on Christmas day it was nearly dark and my bike had no lights.

Christmas was never a big thing at our house and I suppose that's the reason I never really liked it for years after and the reason Donna over compensates and makes Christmas for her family anything but forgetable.

1983 would bring a new chapter in my life. Donna still had contact with dad but as I've already said I'd not seen him for years, this was to change.

Donna had brought a note from dad, it asked Madge could he see me. Madge asked me would I like to see him, I gave it some thought and agreed to go to my gran Karalius' house to meet him.

Walking down the path of 18 Egypt Street that day was one of the scariest things I'd ever done. I'd not been to my gran's house for years and my stomach was turning. I didn't know what sort of reception I was going to get, I did know one thing though, I was about to see my dad again, maybe he would come and watch me playing football just like Ernie White does with his kids. I might even get a proper football kit from him but just like the paint tin incident, my timing was immpecable.

CHAPTER THREE

A Family welcome.

I can't say the welcome that day was the warmest I've ever received, my dad was obviously glad to see me but the rest of them were indifferent. I think they saw me more of a 'Holland' than a 'Karalius' due to the fact that I'd stayed with Madge. My gran, a battleaxe of a woman, she'd been through two world wars and was tough as old boots. She was a similar build to Sarah and was given the nickname 'Ma Baker' by my dad, she was definitely the head of the 'Karalius' clan. She didn't even recognise me and when she was told who I was she just gave a grunt, I didn't know whether it was a grunt of approval or not. Then there was uncle Vin, who refused to speak to me for some weeks. Uncle Brian, the quieter of the three brothers was not bothered one way or the other, my timing could have been better, I expected just my dad and gran being there. Certainly not the whole family with the exception of my dad's sister Mavis.

The name Karalius derives from king Caralus of Lithuania, it was my great grandfather who came over during the First World War with his son 'Vithau,' my granddad. He was killed in a works accident in the 1960's so I never got to meet him, nevertheless they were quite proud of their heritage although none of were actually Lithuanian. My grans maiden name was Conran, which I believe, is of Irish origin.

Gran Karalius died five years ago and I recall going to the house the day of the funeral, it was like a Mafia funeral. All my dads' dodgy mates were there dressed like hit men, it is customary at Lithuanian funerals to stand the open coffin up in the corner. I always thought this to be a bit macabre, so I was relieved to see they'd lay my gran down in the more conventional manner. My wife and I went to kiss her and pay our last respects. As I bent down to kiss her forehead I noticed something, it was the music playing softly in the background, definitely not Lithuanian or Irish. It was of English origin though, in fact it was bad cover version of 'Huey Lewis and the news' Eighties hit 'I'm so happy to be stuck with you.' I looked up at my wife and she was trying her hardest not to laugh. I brought this to my dad's attention and his reply was 'I couldn't find anything Lithuanian.'

I never told Madge how I was treated that day, bloody hell she would have raced down to Egypt Street and wiped the floor with them and that was something none of us needed. I was just glad to see my dad again and didn't really care what the others thought.

Reconciliation seemed to be in the air, Madge had allowed dad to start visiting our house again, his face was a picture when he saw the state it was now in but he didn't say anything, he couldn't. Madge would have told him where to go, he did rehang the doors and started to contribute to my upkeep. Gran Holland must not have approved because this was around the time when things in our house started getting a little spooky.

Dad was building a fort for my soldiers in the living room, it was a good one, everything he did had to be inch perfect. Not a skill I've inherited it must be said, that's probably why I'm sat here writing instead of being out there building things. Madge said she was going to lie down on the bed for an hour, she was up there for about twenty minutes or so when we heard her scurrying down the stairs. She raced into the living room nearly taking the newly hung door back off its hinges, she was white as a sheet.

'What's wrong?' dad asked.

She went on to tell us that she'd just heard gran Holland whistling in the bedroom, gran had a habit of whistling. So nothing unusual then, except for the fact she'd been dead for nearly ten years. Dad scoffed at this and went upstairs to investigate but found nothing untoward.

Several strange things happened at the house and it went on for some years but it wasn't confined just to Sinclair Avenue. I recall being sat in my aunty Pat's house with her and Madge, they were discussing gran and the missing money. When all of a sudden we heard an almighty bang directly above us, we all just sat there looking at each other. Eventually Pat went attentively up the stairs closely followed by Madge. I went and stood in the garden, again just like our house … nothing.

I know what you're thinking, all this can be explained logically and perhaps your right, it can. What happened next though had even the most hardened sceptics speechless.

Aunty Pat was a warden at 'Great Four Acres' a home for physically and mentally handicapped people. Every Christmas they would have a fund raising night, which consisted of Bingo and bring and buy stalls. Madge, Aunty Fiona, Aunty Bella and of course Aunty Pat would always attend as would my gran Holland when she was alive. On this particular night everything went as normal and as the usual pictures were taken by 'The Widnes Weekly News.' One particular photo was taken of Madge and my Aunties in front of the kitchen, each of them holding a champagne glass.

The photo was published in the next issue of the Weekly News, so Aunty Pat went to get copies for everyone else. It wasn't until Pats husband Edwin looked closely at the copies that he spotted something, in the kitchen in the background of the photo there she was clear as day… gran Holland!

As I've previously stated I never felt quite right in that house and would certainly not stay in there on my own under any circumstances. Everyone had their own opinions on why gran wasn't 'at rest' but the general consensus was it must have been something to do with the missing money. Madge speculated on whom she thought had got the money but I'm afraid she took that to the grave with her, as will I.

Now that dad was back on the scene things were getting better. Madge wouldn't stay out as late and certainly wouldn't come home drunk, as my dad used to mind me then and I think deep down she still had feelings for him and maybe she hoped for a full reconciliation with him. This turned out to be false hope, dad was a womaniser and a gambler and I don't think he ever considered to rekindle the flame with Madge. He was at a loose end living with gran Karalius so we'd do for now, until something else came along, something better.

As time passed dad wouldn't come around for weeks and Madge would slip back to her old ways. I was sleeping at the White's again, Madge by now had accepted that dad was not going to change so she too moved on. She announced that she had met someone at the club and would we like to meet him, we agreed. I was expecting a dead head, I'd seen the type of people who drank there.

I accompanied Madge to the club the next Saturday where I would meet this man for the first time. My intention was not to like him, no, to hate him.

'Andrew, this is Al, Al this is my son Andrew.' Madge said.

To my surprise he seemed a really nice man, immaculately dressed and very well spoken, the complete opposite to my dad. Don't get me wrong my dad was also well spoken and quite smart in appearance but with Al it all seemed natural and not contrived. I really liked him.

This was nearly the end of our time in Sinclair Avenue, Madge was soon to move in with Al and although she never gave the house up, we hardly ever stayed there anymore. It was also time for Donna to fly the nest. She moved in with her boyfriend, Peter Conran, does that name ring any bells, it should. It was also the maiden name of gran Karalius, indeed our gran turned out to be Peter's aunty. Which made Donna his second cousin. Nothing wrong with it, try telling Madge that, when she found out Donna was moving in with him the shit hit the fan. I think she would have gone mad who ever it was but given the Karalius connection it just tipped her over the edge.

She'd been drinking and I could see her getting worked up, without a word she dragged me in a taxi to Peter's flat screaming to be let in. Peter opened the door and Madge ran past him and grabbed Donna telling her she was coming home, it got so bad that Peter had to restrain Madge and he eventually calmed her down and made her a cup of coffee. Donna never came home and didn't speak to Madge for some weeks after. Her second cousin is now her husband and the father of my two nieces, so Donna is not only their mum, she's also their fourth cousin twice removed.

Al was to play a substantial part in my life, he didn't have any children and although I don't think he saw me as a son he did a lot more things with me than dad ever did.

His house was as I'd expected, immaculate if somewhat old fashioned. Probably due to the fact it was his mothers house and he had no desire to change it. I was allocated his mothers old room, it was huge. I never liked the idea of sleeping in a dead woman's bed so in an attempt to ease my nervousness I turned over the mattress. I might be in her bed but I definitely wasn't sleeping on the same side mattress as some one who had died, I slept a bit easier that first night and of course left the light on. It wasn't until the next day that Al informed me that he understood that I probably wouldn't like the idea of sleeping in his dead mum's bed so he would get me a new mattress the next week.

'In the mean time I turned the mattress over before you arrived.' He said with a reassuring wink.

Oh my god! I ran up the stairs to 'my' room and turned the mattress back over, my skin felt creepy. I'd shared the same side of a mattress with a dead person.

Al's house was only about three miles from Sinclair Avenue but to me it might as well have been three hundred and I saw my mates less and less.

We spent almost two years with Al and we were well looked after. Madge and Al would spend night after night talking and listening to music, mainly Doctor Hook and The Bee Gees. Every time I hear them even now I'm transported back to Al's house. Particulary one song by Dr Hook *'More like the movies.'* There's a line in it that says. *'You never got to hear those violins...did you girl?'* It's true, I don't think Madge ever heard violins when she was with Al.

I felt lonely in that house but I had my toy soldiers to keep me company. I'd play with them for hours on end and where ever we moved afterwards they came with me. I recall Donna laughing at me for having soldiers up to the age of sixteen, Madge was also concerned, so I would play with them in secret. I don't think they ever quite got it, they weren't just toy soldiers, they were my friends, my escape and they never let me down. They did everything I asked them to do. To this day in times of trouble I sometimes wish I had my old soldiers with me but alas they went to the big battlefield in the sky many years ago.

Dad played a big part in us leaving Al's house. He became jealous of the relationship Madge and I had forged with Al and demanded we moved out. Citing that it wasn't a good environment for me, this was of course bollocks, he just didn't want another man having what he saw was 'his.' He didn't want Madge but he didn't want anyone else to have her either.

It was on a Sunday evening when Al was returning home over some waste land we affectionately know as 'The Bongs' that dad ran up behind Al and hit him over the back of the head with a spanner. Whilst Al lay on the ground dad threatened him that if he carried on seeing me, next time he would kill him. Al was not a fighting man and liked a quiet life and although he never asked us to leave he never put up much of a fight when Madge told him she was going to swap the house in Sinclair Avenue and we would move out.

I think she did this to protect Al because there was no doubt dad would have really hurt him next time and he didn't deserve that.

We briefly moved back to Sinclair while we were waiting for a swap, the house was in even a worse state than when we'd moved out. We slept down stairs for some months, as Madge also didn't feel safe there. We still heard movement and noises upstairs on occasions, nobody was up there, was it gran looking for her money? We'll never know but something was definitely not right there but we had to endure it, where else could we go. Al would still visit and hoped it wouldn't antagonise dad, after all he'd got what he wanted. We were living in a run down house, Al was on his own and dad kept his reputation in tact.

I still went to gran Karalius' house and visited my dad, I wanted to keep him sweet so that he'd leave Madge and Al alone but I was losing the respect I'd always had for him. By now Madge began to hate dad and would have nothing to do with him, instead she reverted to her own 'toy soldiers.' The Labour club, she increased her hours again, the Whites had now moved from Sinclair Avenue so a new place for me to stay at the weekend had to be sorted out. Sometimes I would stay at Donna's or gran Karalius' but mainly I would stay with a family called the Bentleys, this was a perfect arrangement as Keith and Lynda Bentley were regulars at the Labour club and would also stay there until four in the morning. The difference with them was they had five children and they looked after themselves, their ages ranged from nine years of age up to seventeen. I was now nearly thirteen and two of their boys 'Ste' and 'Colin' were of similar age to myself, the other three were girls and I never got on with them.

I hated going to the Bentleys, they lived miles away. Colin was okay but it was quite obvious they, including Keith and Lynda didn't want me there as much as I didn't want to be there but the arrangement would suit them as Madge would ply them with free after hours drinking in return for them minding me. Madge would stay back at Al's at the weekend, I remember thinking how selfish she was for leaving me there.

The Sunday dinners were the worst thing about staying at the Bentleys. Every mouthful of mash potato was filled with lumps, the gravy was like dirty dish water and if you didn't eat it all she would go mad. After having to endure her first dinner I devised a cunning plan … 'Bank bags.' This is not the first time I'd used the bank bag trick to discard unwanted food, it's quite simple, or it would have been. How was I to know that their Yorkshire terrier 'Brandy' was allergic to vegetables.

I'd found myself a nice little spot in the corner of the living room where no one would see my cunning plan in action, my dinner was brought in and while Keith, Lynda and the kids were happily eating their dinners, watching *'Little House on the prairie.'* I had one of my bank bags by my side opened, I would simply scoop the lumpy mash into the bag, close it when it was full and repeat the process until all five bags were full, I had to eat the rest but at least I dodged the mash.

After thanking Lynda for my 'culinary delight' I hid the full bags of mash under my plate, put the plate in the sink and went outside to empty the contents of the bags in the dogs bowl. It went like clockwork, until about an hour after when we heard Lynda let out a loud scream from the back garden. We all ran out to see what was wrong and there he was … Brandy lay on it's back with its legs stuck in the air and lumpy mash coming from his mouth.

'Who give the fucking dog mash?' Lynda screamed.

Everyone turned and stared at me, they all knew the dog had an allergy so it was logical to assume that they wouldn't want to kill their own dog. I didn't want to kill the dog either, I just didn't know.

I never stayed with the Bentleys again much to my relief. I did keep in touch with Colin and he became a good friend of mine until he was hit and killed by a train six years ago. I was sad to hear that, he was a good lad. We even used to laugh years after the event that Brandy probably never had an allergy to vegetables at all but it was more likely he choked on one of the lumps in his mums mash.

Despite the above episode my love for Sunday dinners never diminished. Madge made a mean Sunday dinner but because of that damn club was rarely in a good state to make them so we would go to my gran Karalius' most Sundays. Those are the best memories I have from 18 Egypt Street, her dinners were second to none. The gravy was almost black and was perfectly thick, I would however cover it with red sauce. This always-annoyed gran 'You can't taste the gravy with all that shit on it.' She'd say to me. I loved it and still put red sauce on my Sunday dinner, only now it's my wife who is equally disgusted that I'm ruining the fruit of her labours and tells me so every week.

One particular Sunday all hell broke loose. I heard dad and Vin arguing in the living room, it became louder until eventually they were exchanging punches. I ran in to see what was happening and good enough they were rolling over on the floor. Gran and Brian just carried on watching The Antiques Roadshow as if nothing was wrong. The fight eventually worked its way into the back garden and looked like carrying on all day, suddenly gran Karalius walked into the garden and started hitting them both with a rolling pin. They soon stopped and were reprimanded accordingly. I wouldn't want to mess with her either, I remember thinking. When things calmed and the living room was restored to it's former glory, a loud knock on the front door broke the awkward silence, we all became Emu's, looking around at each other as if to say 'Who's that knocking like that?' The door knocked again and Brian got up to answer, it was the Police. They'd had a report that there was some trouble in the house, gran assured them they must be mistaken, as we'd not long got back from church. They looked puzzled and enquired how Vin had got the cut above his left eyebrow?

'I slipped on a sprout officer.' Was his response.

They of course didn't believe him but what could they do, they had no evidence anything was untoward, so they left.

'That will be those nosy bastards next door who called them.' Dad said nodding his head in the direction of the dividing wall.

Whatever they were fighting over it must have been serious and indeed it was. Vin had six roast potato's and dad only had five, fair enough I thought, you can't short change a man on his roasties.

I related the story to Madge when I got home.

'Is the rolling pin alright?' Was her curt reply.

Madge got an offer of a house swap, it was just up the road from Sinclair Avenue and it was a chance of a new start, she jumped at it.

It was a nice house, exactly the same shape as our old house but it had a good feeling about it. The day arrived for us to move, all the neighbours came to say goodbye, we weren't emigrating for fucks sake. We were moving to the next street, nevertheless, emotions were high. Not so high that anyone offered to help, the only mode of transport at our disposal was Donna and Peter's pea green Austin Maxi. We must of looked like gypsies, I was sprawled on a double mattress in the back of the Maxi holding the back door down, we laughed all the way to Wavertree Avenue and didn't care what people thought. This was a new beginning and we could finally put the past behind us. Al only owned a pushbike but tried to help out where he could and bought Madge some furniture for the new house, as did Donna. I think she was just as excited as Madge was to be making a fresh start. Madge even quit the Labour club, much to everyone's surprise.

Just as we were taking the last bit of furniture from gran Holland's old bedroom, the final weird occurrence took place. On the chimney breast in the room was an old fireplace, it had brittle elements in it, which when lit would generate heat. As we were about to leave the room for the final time the elements fell out of the fire and smashed on the floor.

'Sorry mam … it's time to move on.' Madge said.

Al walked over to the fireplace to pick up the broken elements and as he bent down something inside the fireplace itself caught his eye, it was a letter, or the remains of a letter accompanied by half a dozen or so used matches. It was gran Holland's handwriting but somebody had attempted to burn it and did a good job because we couldn't make out what it said. Madge until the day she died insisted it was a home made will and whoever got gran's money had attempted to burn the evidence. I didn't know if her theory was true and perhaps never will.

The move was finally complete and we were about to shut the door of number 26 Sinclair Avenue for the last time. I was relieved but couldn't help feel a bit sorry for Madge. As she stood in the small hallway at the bottom of the stairs, she looked up to the landing, her eyes filled with tears and with a smile she simply whispered.

'Tara mam.'

CHAPTER FOUR

Should've bought a caravan.

In my relatively short life I have lived at more than twenty addresses. It's only the last ten years or so that I've finally seemed to settle in one place after marrying Louise, my wife. This must be a trait I got from Madge. She would move house frequently after Sinclair Avenue and the new house in Wavertree Avenue, would be the first of three moves in a ten year period.

Life in the new house started out great. Madge's drinking seemed to be confined to weekends when Al would stay over, even then it never got to the point where she'd get in the state she used to get in when she worked at the Labour club. She seemed the happiest I'd seen her for a long time.

The house itself was nice, we had a second hand fake leather corner suite. New carpet and it was always clean. I think she took a lot of pride in it, probably because this was the first house in years she could call her own. Not gran Holland's, not dad's … It was hers.

I was fifteen and had started to take an interest in girls and started to hang around with them as well as the new mates I had acquired because although we'd only moved to the next Avenue, different blocks had different sets of kids. I had defected from the half moon and progressed to the 'Biggie.' The Biggie was so called because it was, well … big, in fact it was about four times bigger than the half moon and it was square. It was the venue for the Silver Jubilee in 1977, that was some day. Although I'm positive the Jubilee was in 1977 there may be some dates and events in this book that may not quite match. Not because I'm lazy, I could easily minimize this page and Google the event to ensure I get the dates correct. But I write as how I remember things. This is not an Encyclopedia that can be used as point of reference for an episode of Eggheads. I still don't doubt for one minute that someone will read this and may find a flaw regarding a date and go to ridiculous proportions to obtain my e-mail address just to inform me I'd got it wrong. Or stop me in the street, and in their best driving examiners voice;

'Actually... I'll think you'll find that The Battle of Waterloo was actually in the October of 1815 and not, as you afore mentioned... The September...' IT'S JUST A BOOK!

Now be honest, how many of you are actually going to put this book down right now and Google what month the The Battle of Waterloo took place? DON'T... I made it up!

The Biggie was the size of a football field. Every blade of grass was filled with row upon row of tables. There were about 500 people from all over the estate and beyond. The atmosphere was electric, everyone wore a union jack in some form or other. There were stalls down one side of the field, selling everything from cakes to patriotic memorabilia. Never one to miss an opportunity, Mrs Harrison had her own stall selling cigarettes. It was the busiest stall there, she must have made a killing. That was the only time I ever saw her smile.

'I don't even like the Queen.' She laughed.

Everyone forgot their troubles for a few hours, even Madge. She was jiving away laughing and singing late into the night. It was good to see her happy. I sat on the grass watching, to my horror she ran over and grabbed my hand. My mates were laughing at me jiving to Glen Miller with my mum. My street cred took a hammering that day.

Most people were there for the festivities alone, this was mainly the case with Madge. I say mainly but she was a complete Royalist, she loved the Queen and the Royal family and our windows were adorned with union Jacks she'd collected from the national newspapers. It's something I've inherited from her, I too am a Royalist, I don't have an affinity with the actual Royal Family itself but I do think we are better served by one, if only to keep the tradition of our great country alive.

There was one member who she never quite took to… Lady Diana, Madge said she never trusted people who couldn't look you in the eye, she even suggested that Diana would eventually bring the Royal Family to it's knees. How true that nearly was.

 Madge had some strange role models, noneother than Margaret Thatcher. Widnes was and still is a staunch Labour town and she was in the minority voting Conservative. She said she admired her stance on the

Falklands conflict and said that a woman would be better equipped to run a country than a man.

I recall being at the fresh meats counter in the Widnes Hypermarket with Madge and a lady asked for half a pound of Corned Beef, which, incidentally came from Argentina. Madge was disgusted and reminded her we had troops risking their lives fighting the Argentinians and we should not endorse any of their products. 'But I like it with a bit of Piccallilli.' The poor lady replied.

Within minutes other people were saying they too would not buy the corned beef. It was withdrawn from their store the day after. Madge was proud of her victory and told everyone that she did her bit for the Falklands conflict.

I look back on the silver Jubilee celebrations and that day in the Hypermarket it always brings a smile to my face. They were good days. Good memories.

Every generation, no matter what era they lived through look back and label them '*The good old days.*'

Gran Karalius was no exception, in fact she was more reminiscent than most. Anyone who would lend her an ear would be told of her exploits as a younger woman.

How during the war she escaped death by inches when the houses across the road were flattened by a German Doodlebug. How they would have to queue for hours for a knob of butter during rationing. And how after the war she would have to walk six miles to do a twelve hour shift spud picking. Then a six mile walk home. She would always end by telling how my grandad was killed in a works accident in the early 60's. She'd then stare into thin air for a few seconds and then came the immortal words; 'Yes, they were the good old days.'

Wavertree Avenue was one of the happiest places we ever lived and this was the first time I learnt a valuable lesson in personal hygiene. Myself and some other kids had decided to climb into the rugby ground for a game of hide and seek. This was one of many games we used to entertain ourselves with. My favorite was 'Arrows.' This consisted of splitting into two teams, the first team would be given some chalk and with a five minute head start would draw arrows on the floor. The second team would then have one hour to catch you up by following the arrows.

I recall on one occasion not having any chalk, so we used a lump of white dog poo instead. Not quite as effective but it did the job. Incidentally what ever happened to white dog poo. You just don't see it anymore.

The rugby ground was a great place for such games. We'd been playing for hours and then sat in the spectators seats pretending to be watching a live game. Naughton Park was in disrepair. It's hard to believe the ground that stands there now. It's a state of the art stadium. This is mainly due to the investment from the Eddie Stobart, Steve O'Connor group, together with the local council they've transformed our little town into somewhere people actually travel to! I quite fancied one of the girls in our gang, Joan, and I got the feeling she liked me, but I wasn't experienced with girls at all and I didn't have a clue where to start. It was apparent that Joan was not backwards in coming forwards. She suggested we should go for a walk around the back of the 'Cow Shed' (an affectionate name given to the home supporters stand) I agreed. I was feeling nervous and was wandering how to initiate the first kiss. I didn't have to, Joan pinned me to the wall and planted her lips squarely onto mine, and it lasted for about a minute. When she finally came up for air she just put her chewing gum back in her mouth looked at me and said;

'Not bad... but your breath smells a bit.'

I ran home and ran to the bathroom, I couldn't find any toothpaste. Madge had false teeth so didn't need it and I hadn't previously been that bothered with my personal hygiene, until now.

I ran into the living room where Madge was sat with aunty Bella and Donna;

'I need toothpaste, quick.' I shouted.

In unison they all looked up at me stood in the doorway like a toothpaste junkie who desperately needed a fix. They all then looked at each other with a sweet smile and said;

'He's met a girl.'

From that day I started to look after myself a bit more. I took a bath at least twice a week and changed my socks at least every three days instead of a week that I previously was used to. I was thirteen years old and thought this was normal. This was also the time I had a brief stint as a male model. Donna was doing a course in fashion at the local college and needed someone to model her latest design. It was normal for me to be Donna's reluctant guinea pig in every new venture she undertook. When she was sixteen she got a job as a Dental nurse and would come home and pull my teeth out. Or the time when she took an interest in hairdressing and cut half off of my hair, leaving the other half so she could go to the Queens Hall disco.

I should have known better this time, but I was a sucker for a new box of soldiers and a Mars bar, so I agreed. I'd been assured no one would recognise me as my hair would be dyed black and I would be wearing black eye liner. This wasn't reassuring me one bit but she'd already bought the soldiers for me and the mars bar was well and truly gone.

The night of the show came and there was I dressed in bin bags cut to the shape of trousers and a pullover looking like a bad David Bowie impersonator. My time to walk down the catwalk came. I pulled it off quite well and I couldn't see anyone I knew, so it didn't turn out that bad. What I didn't cater for was Donna's ridiculous bin bag costume actually winning the competition and me being on page two of the Widnes Weekly News strutting my stuff down the catwalk for all to see.

I was dreading going to school the following Monday morning but I had to face the music. Walking down the corridor to assembly was the worst. Kids wolf whistling at me and singing, 'He's a model and he's looking good.' Their own version of 'Kraftworks' terrible Eighties pop song.

There was an unexpected plus to the whole episode. I'd become quite popular with some of the girls in my year, they'd never even noticed me before but now I was getting quite a bit of attention.

Wavertree Avenue was turning out to be a good move for Madge and myself. It was also the first time I met Margaret Jackson, she was a friend of Madge's. I say friend but Madge met her through my uncle Vin, who Margaret used to live with some years previous. She had moved back to the area after an acrimonious split with a lorry driver in Sheffield and immediately latched on to Madge as she was the only person she knew.

Margaret was quite a character, she was tall with a slim figure for her age and always had her bright copper coloured hair immaculately set in a bouffant style. The poor woman though had a face only a mother could love, she had the biggest nose I'd ever seen, even to this day. It would arrive a good five minutes before the rest of her.

She started to come to our house nearly every day; I could tell she was there by her laugh. She would throw her head back and laugh as loud as she could. At first she was good for Madge, she didn't drink much and was very extrovert. She showed Madge a different way of life that didn't have to involve getting shit faced every weekend. Madge liked her too, even though they were completely opposite to each other. It helped that Margaret was also a fully paid up member of 'KKK', (KILL THE KARALIUS KLAN) having spent many unhappy years with uncle Vin.

It became apparent that Margaret hid a darker side. After a few months she started to become depressed, I couldn't understand why. She was one of the most upbeat people I'd ever met; she would start to sleep at our house, citing that she didn't feel safe on her own. Madge didn't have the heart to tell her she was over staying her welcome. Aunty Bella however did, she sat Margaret down and explained to her that she'd have to go home. Margaret reluctantly agreed and said she'd leave the next day.

The next morning came, I walked down the stairs, through the living room and stopped, something wasn't quite right. As I looked towards the settee where Margaret had been sleeping for the last few weeks, it was empty. She must already have left I thought, not a chance. Upon entering the bathroom to brush my teeth the door wouldn't open fully, something was stopping it, as I looked to see what it was I could just see a head with a huge nose sticking out. It was Margaret lay on the floor next to an empty tablet bottle. I ran up to wake Madge and she frantically ran down and forced her way into the bathroom. Margaret was stretched out on the floor, Madge ran to phone an Ambulance, it was then I noticed something odd, a fly had landed on Margarets face and although she was apparently unconscious, she was wafting the fly away. The ambulance came and took Margaret away and as I suspected she hadn't taken an overdose it was all for attention because she had to leave.

Margaret was admitted to 'Winwick Hospital.' This was a renowned hospital for people with mental problems. She spent seven weeks there but during her stay she would still receive her full state benefits, so when she came out she had over six hundred pounds sat in her bank account. It was a scam, a way of saving money and it became apparent that Margaret had done this several times before. Madge distanced herself from Margaret after that but obviously thought there was some advantages in the 'Winwick' scam as she herself ended up there some months later.

Margaret indeed did have problems, she turned to religion some years later and eventually took her own life... ironically by taking an overdose, maybe not a scam after all, more a cry for help.

I remember being worried about Madge being admitted to Winwick but also in the back of my mind couldn't help thinking that she'd took advantage of the fact that while she was in there she'd be accumulating money. Donna and I went to see Madge almost every day, it was a depressing place, a huge imposing building. On entering you were confronted by a long white corridor with doors on either side. The further up the corridor we went the louder the noise became. The sound of people whining, screaming and crying, why anyone would stay in this madhouse voluntarily was way beyond me. I was pleased that when we got to the end of the corridor we turned right as most of the noise was coming from the left, that, apparently was where the real mental cases were kept. Madge was in a ward of about fifteen people, they all looked fine to me, maybe this 'scam' was more widespread than I initially thought. Tell the doctor you're depressed, get prescribed anti-depressants and tell him they not working then get admitted to Winwick for a few weeks while still getting you're benefits, job done. Fuck me I wish Winwick was still there, I could do with a rest myself.

One particular visit sticks out in my mind. Donna and I had visited Madge and were preparing to leave. The sky was black and the rain started, rain like I'd never seen. We stood in the foyer waiting for our opportunity to run to the car. Finally we braved the elements and got to the car but it wouldn't start, the starter motor was jammed. Mobiles were not in wide use those days so we had to run back to the building to phone the AA recovery vehicle. They told us to wait for half an hour, again we stood in the foyer looking at the horrendous weather when a voice came from behind us;

'Oh dear, my daughter will never be able to pick me up in this weather.' A lady of about sixty stood behind us dressed in a fur coat and wooly hat. She explained she'd been visiting her sister and was getting picked up by her daughter who lived in Runcorn, the next town to us but was afraid she wouldn't be able to make it because of the weather. Donna told her it would be no trouble for us to drop her off as it wasn't much out of our way. We stood chatting until the recovery vehicle came and fixed the car. The rain had eased off somewhat and the old lady was about to get in the back of the car when two nurses ran out and told us they'd been looking for her. It turns out the old lady was a patient and her daughter had died some years earlier sending her into depression.

Winwick Hospital was knocked down ten years ago and in its place stands a brand new housing estate, on occasions I pass by and always look up to the sky and recall that day Donna and I nearly assisted an involuntary breakout.

Madge was in hospital for five weeks and came home to a nice sum of money, she seemed really upbeat and even bought a new video recorder. A Betamax, it was massive but I didn't care, we were moving up in the world. Donna took me to rent some videos and Madge and I sat and watched

'Escape to victory' followed by 'The life of Brian' with our Sunday dinner on our laps. It was a great day, I ate my dinner and went to go out the door to play football with my mates, as I got to the door Madge shouted me back;

'What mum?' I asked.

With a smile she looked up at me and said;

'I love you son.'

I never doubted that.

'The life of Brian' was very appropriate. We were playing football in the street when I saw a man walk past me in a trance like state. He was carrying a house brick, he then threw the brick through Mr. Twiggs car windscreen and calmly walked away. We all stood there in amazement at what we'd just witnessed. I was even more amazed because when I looked again I recognised him, it was Uncle Brian. Mr. Twigg ran out of the house and overheard me tell my mates I recognised the man. I ran home to tell Madge what had just happened. I was there not five minutes when a loud knock came on the door. It was the Police.

It turns out Mr. Twigg, a neighbour of ours and my mate Jimmy's dad, was seeing a woman called Nancy. Nancy was an ex-partner of my uncle Brian's, she'd ended their relationship some months earlier. Uncle Brian wouldn't accept it and declared war on Mr. Twigg. Unlike my dad, a house brick through a car window was the extent of Brian's wrath.

Brian had an unlucky life by all accounts. Madge told me how he was jilted at the alter by the love of his life 'Rose,' he never got over it and lived with gran Karalius all his life.

When the police were trying to force me to give evidence against Brian, Madge was reluctant to let me. Not just because she feared any reprisals from my dad, but she genuinely liked Brian, he was a decent sort. Dad and Vin were tough and had reputations and were not afraid to bend the law. Brian was the straight man of the family and Madge really felt sorry for him, in any case she didn't even like Mr. Twigg.

The police got what they wanted, they threatened Madge if she didn't allow me to give evidence they would sopina her. She later wrote a short letter to dad explaining that we didn't want to give evidence against Brian but were given little choice.

The dreaded day finally arrived. Madge and I were sat in the foyer at Warrington Crown Court, when in walked Brian accompanied by my dad. They both looked at Madge and smiled, she just shook her head, almost apologetically. We were next in court and my stomach was turning, I felt sick, it was then that everything I'd been told about Brian was confirmed. A policeman called us into a room and sat us down, he had a smile on his face. He informed me that I wouldn't have to give evidence after all. When Brian saw me he said he couldn't put me through such an ordeal, so he changed his not guilty plea to guilty…result, you may think. Not really, he got twelve months in prison, as the brick incident was the latest in a long campaign against Mr. Twigg. For the first time in my life I felt real guilt, I felt like a traitor. My involvement, no matter how reluctant had sent my own uncle to prison.

I myself wrote a letter to Brian in prison, again telling him how sorry I was. True to form he written back to me, telling me it was not my fault and he felt bad for involving me in the first place. He did have one request though, his final line read;

'Life's hard and throws things at you that you don't expect. That's when you need your family around you. Go and see your dad, he misses you.'

Uncle Brian died two years ago. Dad and I were left with emptying the house in Egypt Street, as he was the last occupant remaining. He was born there and that house was a Karalius house for over seventy years. I stood in the empty shell of the living room and realised how Madge must have felt leaving Sinclair Avenue, the end of an era. What was once a vibrant house was now going to be given to another family, a new dynasty, where they could make their own memories. 'Lets go then.' Dad said clearing his throat.

'Are you alright dad?' I asked. He looked at me and said;

'Life goes on.'

He shut the door one last time and never looked back. That day was when I realised dad was human, he'd been crying, of course he wouldn't admit it and I never mentioned it either…life goes on!

After Brian's letter I got back in touch with dad and again started visiting gran's house, some good came out of the house brick saga after all. As for our time in Wavertree Avenue, that was coming to an end. Madge was getting itchy feet and felt another fresh start was what the doctor ordered. I couldn't understand why, on the whole we were happy there.

It became apparent the reason for Madge wanting to move was to be close to Aunty Bella. The new house would back on to hers, they were always close. I understood this but didn't want to move from my friends again. Madge asked me to come and look at the house, it was in a suburb of Widnes, an area known as 'Ditton.' Ditton was about three miles from

Wavertree Avenue and once more I'd have to start all over again. Aunty Bella's son Tony lived there, there was a four months age gap between us and we grew up together, so I had a start, someone to hang out with.

I still wasn't keen. Until I saw the house, it was so different than anywhere I'd ever lived before. As opposed to the pre-war solid brick houses of Sinclair and Wavertree, Parbold court was a terrace, one of ten in a row, half new brick half dark timber, opposite was a mirror image, a row of ten houses. Each house had a small open garden separated only by ten individual paths all leading to one communal path running through the middle. Every door was open and on every open garden kids young and old were playing, parents were laughing and popping in and out of each other's houses. I'd never experienced so much sense of community before, yes there was the Jubilee celebrations of '77 but that was a one off. Before we even got in the house people were telling Madge how nice it was living there. Ditton had and still does have a poor reputation but it was growing on me. On entering the house we were confronted by a long hallway with the living room off to the left and a big open back kitchen at the end of the hallway. What would be my bedroom was twice the size of any I'd previously had, there was a shed at the bottom of the garden, it was perfect. The couple who wanted to swap with Madge said they'd leave all the carpets, this was a two-bed house and Wavertree was a three bed, they had a young family and were in need of more bed space. After looking around the house Madge asked me what I thought, before I could answer she played her trump card.

'Aunty Bella is giving one of her dogs away, I thought 'Duke' would be perfect for this garden... well?' She said with a smile on her face.

I'd always wanted a dog, yes it was somewhat of a bribe.... but I've always been a bit partial to a bribe, anyway I loved the place. It was agreed, the swap would take place in the next fortnight. I was no longer a 'Townie.' I was about to become 'Dittoner.'

There were no such dramatics having to leave Wavertree as there was with leaving Sinclair. We'd only lived there just over eighteen months and had no real affinity with the house, in fact we were excited about moving again.

When Madge went to the council office to sign the papers confirming the swap it was the same woman who dealt with the move from Sinclair;

'Moving again Mrs. Holland... you should've bought a caravan.'

CHAPTER FIVE

COMING OF AGE.

Our time as 'Dittoners' began really well. Madge was a lot happier. She even got a job in the local crisp factory making 'Golden Wonder' crisps. Our house was full of crisps and Pot noodles. I can't look at a pot noodle now without feeling sick. The factory used to sell them to the workers half price, so everyone would stock up on them. I saw this as an opportunity, I would get as many bags of crisps and pot noodles as I could at half price and sell them to a chippy located one hundred yards from our house at three quarter-price, everyone's a winner. Or at least they would have been. The reason the factory sold them half price was they were past the shelf life.

The chippy was closed down for a week for selling out of date food. Luckily for me they never told anyone where they got them. I felt really bad about the closure, it was a great chippy. A real hub of the community, it was the type of chippy where people would take their own plates and the staff would fill them up. Just like when I was a kid. Sadly those chippy's have died off over the years. With one exception… Marie Barrow's. A small and basic English chippy just outside the town centre but the food is second to none. They only open at dinner times and Thursday and Friday teatime. Even now I go there most weeks, we still call Friday in our house Marie's night. If you ever find yourself in our sleepy little town, ask someone where Marie Barrow's chippy is? Everyone knows it, then go and sample some of the best food the north has to offer. It'll be the one with the queue around the corner but I promise you… it's worth the wait.

That was a short-lived venture, but never dampened my appetite for making a couple of quid here and there.

Despite the fact school was now a bus ride away as opposed to the five minute walk it used to be when we lived at Wavertree, I attended more regularly, mainly due to the fact that I was taking a lot more interest in girls and they in me. This was also the time I discovered I enjoyed writing. Mr. Kirwin was my English teacher, he was cool as teachers went and encouraged my 'talent', as he called it. I won three writing competitions in one term. There was one teacher I particularly disliked, Mr. Hollitt. I had good reason, my sir name 'Karalius' is a famous name in rugby league, nothing to do with me, my dads cousin Vin (not to be confused with my uncle Vin) played for Wigan amongst others and also represented Great Britain at the highest level. He acquired the nickname 'The wild bull of the pampas' due to his robust style of play. I only ever saw him at family weddings, but this made no difference to Mr. Hollitt. He was a big imposing welsh man, bald with a bushy beard inspiring us to nickname him 'Upside down head.' He never knew this, had he, we would have endured the wrath of his 'Golden Golly,' a size fourteen golosher, deliberately painted red underneath to indicate blood. That was the type of man he was, a bully. Being Welsh he was a huge fan of rugby, so for a short time I was his favorite, my name was Karalius, I must be a rugby genius like my second cousin. Not a bit, I hated rugby and loved football. Nevertheless he would still put me on the team sheet just to let the other team know they had a legendary name in our side.

It took him three months to realise I was shit. He took this personally and made my PE lessons hell, he knew I loved football so would look for any excuse for me to miss out and run around the field for the whole lesson. I swear to god whilst taking the register, he shouted my name out, I replied 'Yes sir' and he made me run and miss football, for answering back. Next lesson I decided not to answer to my name and the bastard made me run throughout the lesson for being ignorant.

Despite his best efforts I made the football team. We were quite good, mainly due to the fact that apart from me, the other ten players were scousers. They all came from Hale village, they had to attend our school by coach, even though they lived on the outskirts of Liverpool they were one mile too far outside the catchment area to qualify for a Liverpool school, so they had to come to our school in Widnes. They hated that, I think it made them feel less 'Scouse.' We of course reminded them of this on a daily basis. Apart from usually being gifted at football, they have another gift, more of a quirk. They have an inability to calling people by their first names and they add a 'Y' or an 'O' to surnames, I think this is unique to Scousers. Let me give you an example, this was a typical team sheet for our football team;

Murpho
(Murphy)

Mainey Keeno Bammo Matty
(Maine) (Keane) (Bampton) (Mathews)

Pazzy Jacko Aspy Danno
(Parry) (Jackson) (Aspinall) (Daniels)

Krailo Robbo
(Karalius) (Robson)

Why they do this has always been a mystery to me, when someone actually calls them by their correct name, they become confused. Some of the names above are all I remember them by, I can't honestly remember most of their first names, one I do remember is Keeno, everytime his name was shouted out in register it was always followed by the whole class trying their hardest not to laugh, 'Archibald Keen.' No wonder he preferred Keano.

The worst teacher at Wade Deacon High School was, without doubt the Head Mistress, Miss Johnson, she was hard to put an age on. She was medium build with short reddy-brown hair. She had a face like a Bulldog chewing a wasp. She always wore the same sort of clothes, a blazer, pencil skirt and black flat shoes and would stand with her hands behind her back. She introduced some very strange schooling methods. Most schools were singing normal Hymns in morning assembly, not us. We were singing 'If I had a hammer' and 'Swing bell over the land.' Even the teachers found it a bit odd. The most insane thing she added to the curriculum was, Ballroom dancing. Today that might be quite cool given the resurgence of Ballroom but in the 80's it was just fucking stupid and made us look idiots. Especially with St Josephs, our neighboring school and our archenemies. Every year our two schools would have an annual scrap on the shared sports field. When they found out we did Ballroom they refused to come out and fight us, in case we asked them to do a 'Quick step.' It was embarrassing. The hard earned reputation our school had built up over the generations had been shattered with one cutting remark.

The Ballroom lesson itself was mortifying. The boys would have to ask the girls would they like to dance. The trick was not to ask the good-looking girls, if they didn't fancy you, they would say no and make you look a right fool. You didn't want to be left with the mingers either, you had to ask the middle of the road girls.... just to save face. We were fourteen, it was wrong on every level.

Miss Johnson acquired the nickname 'Hitler.' It was while we were queuing up to go into a Math's lesson that she was walking past and somebody shouted out to her Hitler. She stopped in her tracks, about turned and walked right up to myself and three of my mates. It wasn't even us who shouted it, that didn't matter.

'My office, now.' She said in her quiet but stern manner.

She stood us all in a line in her office and walked up and down, demanding she wanted to know who'd shouted Hitler. We were genuinely scared, she was an imposing woman. We were all standing with our hands behind our backs, heads bowed, when all of a sudden we noticed 'Piggy Williams's' socks.... he had half mast trousers and wore one bright pink sock and one bright green. We all lost it and started giggling, to all our surprise Miss Johnson made a Karate stance and started kicking out like Bruce Lee. We ran out of her office with her running after us down the corridor. We all got suspended for two-weeks. It was worth it, it was hilarious. Apart from that I was doing quite well at school.

I think the progress I was making at school was down to my home life. I was taking more responsibility for myself. Ditton was quite a rough area and you had to know how to look after yourself, it's a time in my life I look back at with a smile, there weren't enough hours in the day. I'd go to school, come home and rush my tea, get changed and go to the Youth club I'd started attending. I owe a lot to that place, it taught me a lot, not all good it must be said.

Madge had made new friends because no sooner had we moved to Ditton, Aunty Bella had moved closer to town, nothing personal she assured Madge.

Directly across from our house lived Maggie Walters, she had five young boys and she and her estranged husband would provide the neighbours with no end of entertainment most weekends. Like clockwork, twelve thirty every Friday or Saturday night he would go to the house, drunk as a skunk declaring his undying love for Maggie, she in turn would open the bathroom window and throw a bowl of water over his head, at least I think it was water. He never learnt, every time the same. He would stagger off dripping wet slurring the words of the Andy Williams hit 'I love you baby.'

Madge, I think saw something of herself in Maggie and they become friends. The only problem was, Maggie was an alcoholic. Her preferred drink was sherry. Madge would spend hours at Maggie's house and would stagger home in the early hours. It cost her job at the crisp factory. This was not so much a problem for me. I was leading my own life and was soon to be confronted with my own alcohol demons.

Aunty Bella was also divorced, unlike Madge and my dad, they were still good friends. Uncle Archie was a quiet hard working sort, he never swore. Aunty Bella was out going and almost the complete opposite to Archie. Bella moved out of the marital home and Archie stayed in the four bed-roomed house on his own. Tony and I, were still very close, especially now we lived in Ditton and Archie's house in Montgomery Road was less than a minutes walk from our house. Tony would stay with him at weekends. He had a key to the house and we would often go there while Archie was at work and raid his cupboards, he never minded, I suppose he was grateful that he wasn't the only one rattling about in the once busy and vibrant house.

Although I was doing a lot better at school, Tony and I would occasionally bunk off and use Archie's house as refuge. We never did it often enough t arouse any suspicion. One fateful Friday afternoon we made a mistake, a mistake that may have been the biggest of my life. This is when I tasted real alcohol for the first time.

Archie liked a drink and made his own Bitter, he brewed it in a shed in the back garden. Tony was more street-wise than I and had convinced me his dads home brew was nice, besides who'd know if we took a pint or two each. Trouble was we had four or five each. Anyone who has ever tasted home brew would tell you how strong it tastes and the effects four or five pints could have, particularly to someone who'd never had a drink before.

I remember struggling with the first glass it tasted awful. After that I didn't much care. I left Archie's house and attempted the short walk home, Madge probably was in Maggie's house and wouldn't even notice I'd not been to school. I don't recall that short walk, the air hit me and that was it, I was well and truly pissed. I do recall entering the house. I was about to put the key in the door when Madge opened it. I fell flat on my face in the hallway, I looked up and there stood Madge and Aunty Fiona, she'd called in for a rare visit. She stood there, arms folded and said;

'You've not been to school, have you?'

'And what are you goin' sho aboush it... I'm not sheven any more.' I drawled back at her staggering to my feet.

She smacked me across the head. Madge ordered me upstairs and all I remember as I was staggering up the stairs was aunty Fiona's voice;

'To think, I saved that little bastards life.'

Uncle Archie's house was not the only time I was to experience something for the first time. It was also the venue where I was about to lose my virginity, or so I thought.

We'd been to a disco at the community centre until ten O'clock, Archie was on nights, Tony had invited two girls back to his dads' house. I won't name them but lets just say they had a reputation. I'd just turned fifteen and was ready to become a man.

Only one problem, I was shitting myself. Tony had informed me we didn't need to woo these girls in any way, they were easy. That made it worse, these girls were obviously experienced and I was definitely not. My reputation could be in tatters before I'd had time to establish one. We sat in the living room with a bottle of cider, the girls were whispering to each other and giggling. Tony was the perfect host, he'd been here before, he was much more adept than I. He nodded his head in my direction and asked me to come to the back kitchen for a minute.

'Which one do you want?' He asked.

'They're both mingers, I don't want any.' I replied.

Of course I was lying. They weren't the best looking girls in the world but they weren't mingers either. I just didn't know how to 'do it.' Tony sensed this and laughed. He assured me everything would be fine. We entered the living room and Tony summoned one of the girls upstairs. I was left with the other one, the palms of my hands were sweaty and I could feel my heartbeat in my head. She shuffled over to the end of the settee leaving enough room for me to sit next to her. I walked over to the light switch and turned the lights off. I sat down next to her and we started kissing, her breath smelt of cider and cigarettes but I was getting aroused.

I plucked up the courage to put my hand up her top when the lights came on. It was Archie, he'd been sent home from work ill. 'Jesus, Mary and Joseph.' That's as bad as Archie's language ever got, before running up the stairs shouting for Tony.

We made a sharp exit and Archie took the key off Tony. I was relieved we got caught but also felt a bit disappointed. Tony's well-built reputation took a knock. The next night in the youth club, he asked a girl out and she just looked at him and said with an air of teenage sarcasm;

'Will ya dad be there?' Tony had blonde hair so when he blushed he looked like a tomato.

Everyone burst into laughter, Tony replied in the only way he knew how;

'Slag.' And walked off to play table tennis.

Not long after I was made to go and apologise to Aunty Fiona for my behaviour the day I got drunk. I didn't want to, I could only remember her amongst others, rifling through grans' house after she died. For Madge's sake, I reluctantly agreed.

She'd already been informed I was coming, so I couldn't even pretend I'd been to Madge. Fiona would have been on the phone in an instant with the opening immortal line of 'Madge, I don't want to get Andrew in trouble, but....'

I had to bite the bullet and go back to Sinclair Avenue for the first time in a long time. I got off the bus at the front end of the rugby ground and began to walk the two-minute or so walk to Sinclair. As I turned into the Avenue there were kids of about ten or eleven years old playing football on the half moon, that was me not so long ago. It all looked so small, how did we play on it but then I realised, the field was the same size as it always was, I'd just got bigger. As I passed number 26 I felt a tinge of sorrow. The house was unrecognisable, the new occupants had painted the front of it red.

How dare they, that was our house. I then crossed over towards Sarah's old house, that too had changed, the garden had been cultivated and a young girl played in it. I stopped and looked again at the kids playing football, then at number 26. Fuck it, I thought, why should I apologise to her. I'm not a baby anymore, so I about turned and walked back to the bus stop.

I was disappointed at the change in Sinclair Avenue. I suppose I still thought everything would be the same, but like we all have to accept, people move away, people die and life goes on.

When I arrived back at our house, Donna and Peter were there. I was glad, Donna would be moral support. Madge immediately asked me how it went with Aunty Fiona. I grumbled and went through to the back kitchen. Donna had come with the news that her and Peter were to be married. Donna asked how I felt, I was fifteen, I didn't care. Madge took the news well, I don't think she was warming to Peter but she was starting to accept that he wasn't going away. She couldn't resist getting a sly dig in though.

'At least the buffet won't cost that much, you've both got the same families.'

Donna went to say something but Peter shook his head to her indicating she should leave it. I suppose they expected a worse reaction than that. It was later that evening after a bottle of sherry at Maggie's house, her true feelings about the impending wedding would come to light. I came home from the youth club at about ten thirty, to find our house in total darkness. I went across to Maggie's, as I walked in I could smell the sickly odour of 'Harvey's Bristol Cream.' All Maggie's children were sat around, the younger ones in just their nappies. Her house was shabby, as was Maggie. The years of drinking were taking its toll. She must only have been in her early Forties but you could add at least ten years on her appearance but she was a lovely woman and like Madge, she'd just fell on hard times. Madge was slumped in the chair with the now familiar glass of sherry. I asked her for the key, she looked up at me and told me to go and live with my fucking sister as I approved of her marriage to Peter. I informed her I wasn't bothered either way but it fell on deaf ears. She had 'Madge eye syndrome,' I hadn't seen that look for years and I didn't like it.

I got the key and went home to bed. A couple of hours later my bedroom door was pushed open and there stood Madge, angrier than ever and accusing me again of being pro-Donna and Peter. I got dressed and slept in the shed, I say slept but I never got a winks sleep, it was freezing. At about 4.30 am, I quietly climbed through the back kitchen window and put my head around the living room door. Madge was sprawled on the couch, fully clothed. Not for the first time, I went upstairs to get a blanket and covered her up, like I said it was a cold night.

Just like Sinclair, the next morning was like nothing had happened. I got up about dinnertime and went down stairs, Madge was watching telly.

'Put the kettle on son.'

She never apologised, that used to irritate me but I think she was embarrassed. I made a cup of tea and took it in to her. As I sat down I simply said to her;

'I didn't go to Aunty Fiona's mum.'

She looked over at me, took a sip of her tea and said;

'I know son.'

An opportunity came for me to go on holiday with one of my new mates, John Wilson. His mum and dad owned a caravan in Towyn, North Wales. Madge didn't have any money for my spends so I went to see my dad, I was told by uncle Brian he was away on business, in actual fact he was serving three months in Walton prison for handling stolen goods. Brian gave me thirty pounds for my holiday. Madge got twenty pounds together and off I went. I'd just have to take it easy with what little money I had.

Fifty pounds was a substantial amount of money for a fifteen year old but I was there for two weeks and that gave me less than five pounds a day. I was conscious of it but not to worried, I was determined to have a good holiday.

What happened next epitomized what Madge was all about, especially without the booze. I was only in Towyn for three days when a knock came on the caravan door, John's mum answered it and told who ever it was to come in... It was Madge. I couldn't believe my eyes, she said she'd come for a day out with Aunty Bella and thought she'd see how I was doing. I asked where Bella was and she said she'd left her playing bingo on the sea front. She commented how lovely the camp was and would I show her around before she had to leave. We went to the cafe on the camp, as we sat there she held out her hand, in it was fifty one-pound notes rolled up in an elastic band.

'You don't think I was going to let you scrimp and scrape did you?' She said.

I asked was she really with Aunty Bella and she assured me she was and that they'd got here in Bella's eldest daughters car. Madge looked at the clock on the wall and had a drink of her tea and said she was running late to meet Bella. She kissed me on the forehead and told me to have a great holiday and that she would see me when I got home.

I went to go back to the caravan, I was pleased that I now had enough money to fully enjoy my holiday. I changed my mind, instead of going back to the caravan, I'd decided to go to the arcade on the sea front and spend a bit of my newfound wealth. As I turned the corner I saw Madge stood at the bus stop, before I could shout her a bus pulled up and she got on. As the bus drove away I saw Madge walk down the aisle and take a seat at

Madge

the back. I felt guilty. To get to Towyn from Widnes she would have had to take four busses and a train.

I never told her I knew what she'd done but that one thing always sticks in my mind, seeing that bus pull away. Her love may not always have been apparent, but it was there nevertheless. The holiday itself was not the best I've ever been on, mainly because I never got on too well with John, he had money and knew I didn't and he'd flaunt it at every opportunity. It's sad what money can do to people, there have been times in my life when I've had money and times when I've had nothing but I've never let that influence how I see other people, no matter what their monetary status.

Ditton, as I've already stated, was a rough area. I came back from Towyn to find there had been a spate of burglaries on our estate. At least we had Duke not very menacing looking but a deterrent by way of his bark if nothing else. Madge would leave Duke in the house if we were not going to be in. One evening we arrived home at about nine-thirty after visiting Bella's house. As we walked up the path Madge noticed there was a light on in the hall, she was pretty sure she'd not left it on before we left. We both stood still half way up the path. I took out my key and put it in the lock, I looked back at Madge one last time before I entered. As I opened the door and entered the hallway, all I could see was things all over the floor, clothes, ornaments. I ran into the back kitchen, then the living room, the same. We had been burgled, there was no one there. The bastards had long gone, taking our video recorder and anything else of any value with them. Madge was distraught, so much for our guard dog, we looked everywhere but couldn't find him. I heard a noise upstairs, I was annoyed and lost any fear I previously had. I ran up the stairs armed with a kitchen knife but could see nothing. I heard movement again in Madge's bedroom, as I stood in the doorway it appeared the noise was coming from under her bed.

'Come out you bastards.' I shouted.

A head popped out from under the bed, it wasn't a human head, it was Duke. He'd been hiding from the burglars. Despite my anger I couldn't help but smile, just our luck, a guard dog that hides from burglars. He probably made them a cup of tea for fucks sake.

We didn't have any home insurance, so everything that was stolen had to be replaced but that takes money and we didn't have much of that. There was one small consolation. The burglars didn't have the time or the know how to break into the gas meter, which worked off fifty pence pieces. It was due to be emptied and was quite full. Maggie, being much more street-wise than Madge spotted this straight away. She explained to Madge that she should break into the meter herself, take what ever was in it and blame it on the burglars before she called the Police. Madge wasn't one to break the law and was reluctant but I wasn't. I ran to the shed and got a hammer and chisel and proceeded to break into the meter.

'Stop.' Maggie shouted, she handed me a pair of odd socks that had been left in the aftermath of the burglary from the hall floor and told me to put them on my hands.

'Finger prints.' She said.

She'd obviously done this before. I placed the chisel against the gas meter and raised the hammer above my head, as I did I heard a growl coming from behind me. It was Duke.

'Now your a guard dog.' I said with an air of irony.

I then raised the hammer in Dukes direction and again he whimpered and ran upstairs and hid under Madge's bed.

There was almost £200 pounds in the meter, all in fifty pence pieces, the only problem was how to get it all changed without arousing any suspicion. Had we still lived in Wavertree this would have indeed have been a problem but this was Ditton and Maggie knew exactly where to go. She took me to meet Clive. He was a black guy and was notorious, if not a legend in Ditton, he lived just two blocks away from our house, I'd seen him a few times at the youth club but never spoke to him. Maggie knocked on the door of his mum's house and Clive answered.

'Yeah.' He said with a menacing look.

Maggie explained our problem regarding the fifty-pence's. He stood and started to comb his Afro, he looked up and down the street and invited me in. Maggie scurried down the path and went home. Clive told me he would change the silver for me but he wanted ten percent. I had no choice, so I agreed. There was £196 in total, so ten percent would have £19.60. He then shouted his mum into the living room and told he needed £186.00 in notes. To my surprise she was white. She was dripping in gold. She went off and came back with the money Clive had requested. He in turn handed me the money and told me not to tell anyone where I'd got it from.

'You've took ten pounds.' I told him very politely.

Again he looked at me menacingly, put his head closer to my face and snarled;

'Like I said, ten percent. If you don't like it... fuck off.'

I explained to him that the ten pounds he'd took was closer to five percent and he should have took closer to twenty pounds, which would have been ten percent.

He moved his face closer still to mine and said less menacingly than before;

'Are you saying I'm thick?'

'Yeah, are you saying he's thick.' Said his mum, in a broad scouse twang.

I told them I appreciated what they'd done for me and didn't want them to lose out on the deal by making what was obviously a rare mistake. They accepted my explanation in good faith, deducted another ten pounds and sent me on my way. I wasn't going to haggle over the forty pence they owed me, I was just glad to get out of the house in one piece.

When I gave Madge the money, she took it but I could tell she didn't like the idea of how we got it. It at least paid for the window the bastards broke in the back kitchen door and left £150.00 to replace the television and video recorder.

Madge was a bad liar and when the police were called and asked her basic routine questions, she nearly buckled. I thought she was going to confess all. Again Maggie stepped in and told them she was upset and shaken up. They said they understood, left an incident number and went on their way. Maggie took Madge to her house for a glass of sherry; 'Just one or two, for the shock.' She whispered to me.

We'd lived in Ditton for only a short time but already I'd tasted alcohol for the first time, had my first proper encounter with a girl and been involved in my first criminal activity. It was hard to imagine I was the same boy from Sinclair Avenue. I was becoming more streetwise. For better or for worse, I had changed and was definitely, coming of age.

CHAPTER SIX

CHIP OFF THE OLD BLOCK.

    I attended Ditton Youth Club Monday to Friday, with the exception of Wednesdays, that night as allocated to juniors. I was becoming well liked and quite a proficient pool and table tennis player. The girls would always congregate around the pool table and it gave me plenty of opportunity to show off. I'd made new friends and didn't have to rely on our Tony anymore for confidence. Mike Rigby, Cal Birchall and Ste Bradley, otherwise known as, Rigger, Cal and Brad. We had become inseparable. We met through our love of table tennis and formed one half of the youth club table tennis team.

    Our backgrounds were chalk and cheese, Rigger was one of three boys and lived with his mum and dad. They were a working class family and had a nice house but I always remember clothes being strewn all over the place. He claimed his house was haunted, he said his dead grandmother used to stand over his bed some nights and just watch him. I never doubted him, how could I after my own experiences. It was in his house I thought I'd seen a ghost, one afternoon I'd called to Riggers house, it was between 12:30 and 1 pm, I can say that with confidence because as he let me in, he told me to go and wait for him in the living room while he got a shower. I sat watching 'The Sullivan's' (an Australian soap of the day, it was aired between the above times) as I sat waiting, half watching the television, I saw something in the corner of my eye. It was an old woman, quite a big woman probably in her Eighties. She just stood at the doorway between the living room and kitchen trying to catch her breath. My blood ran cold, she looked normal, alright maybe a bit pale on reflection but definitely not dead. I heard Rigger coming down the stairs, I was relieved. Rigger walked in drying his hair with a towel, he looked up at the old lady stood in the doorway and calmly said;

'Alright gran.'

I know he said he'd seen her a few times but this was just fucking weird. He looked at me and must have seen my face, the penny dropped and he started to howl with laughter. It transpires that the old lady was indeed his gran but not his dead gran. This was his dads' mum who lived across the back and had come over to collect her dinner that Riggers mum prepared for her everyday. How was I to know, he'd never mentioned he had two grans' and one was alive and kicking. It was all a misunderstanding but brought no end of entertainment for his mum and dad every-time I visited their house.

Cal and Brad lived on the same block, an affluent area directly across from the youth club. Cals' mum and dad were in their late fifties, they had Cal relatively late in life. They were more like his grandparents, they had a few bob but were very down to earth. It was Cals' house that we used as the venue for Subbuteo tournaments. For those who have never played Subbuteo, you've never lived. It's a game where you flick little footballers at an oversized football, the object is the same as real football, whoever scores the most goals wins. We took it quite serious and made every Wednesday night 'Subbuteo night.'

I even painted my own Brazil kit on these tiny figures, it took over ten painstaking man-hours to paint them. They were so small I had to use a needle. It was all worth it when I beat Brads' Argentina on penalties in the world cup final. I know what your thinking, we really needed to get out more but it was fun.

Brads' house was more conventional, his mum and dad were quite young and insisted we called them by their first names. We often use to wind Brad up saying that Rigger fancied his mum and that the feeling was mutual, it drove him mad.

Every Saturday night we would sleep at my house. Madge would buy us some cans of lager, Brad would bring his Atari and we were set for the night.

This coincided when newly formed Channel 4 used to air 'The red triangle films.' The red triangle in the top right hand corner of the screen indicated adult viewing only, we were nearly sixteen, that was adult enough for us. The films were sexually explicit, we would turn the volume down so Madge couldn't here what we were watching. At first we would all in turn disappear to the toilet for a couple of minutes, it became clear what

everyone was doing. One particular night Rigger, never one to hide his light under a bushel, got out his penis and started masturbating under the blanket. We all looked at him, he stopped for a moment and said;
'What? It's what you all go to the toilet for anyway.'

He had a point, so we all followed suit. Being competitive, whether it is Pool, Table Tennis or Subbuteo we decided to have a wanking race... Rigger won every time.

One particular night we were 'racing' away when all of a sudden Madge walked in, we all stopped and looked at her. I don't know who was more mortified, Madge or us. She apologised and made a quick exit.

We never spoke about that night. Madge definitely never mentioned it and our sleepovers became less frequent.

Tuesday night at the youth club was table tennis match night, we were due to play away at a venue in Runcorn, to our horror when we arrived all the opposing team were disabled and were in wheelchairs. We didn't know what to do, I for one didn't want to play. If I won I'd feel bad, if I lost I'd feel even worse losing to someone in a wheelchair. That night I learned a valuable lesson, one that stays with me to this day.

My name was called out, I was next on. I played at only about fifty per cent and lost the first game. I was getting beat one game to nil in a best of three match. Olive, our coach was about fifty or so and had played at County level in her younger days, she knew her way around the table. She called for a time out. She could see I wasn't enjoying my game, she asked me why I was playing so bad?

I told her I didn't enjoy playing somebody who was handicapped.

'How would you play to win against an able bodied person?' She asked.

'What do you mean?' I replied.

She went on to explain that these people chose to play in an able bodied league and would feel patronised if we didn't play our best game against them. I should use their weakness to win, place the ball where they can't reach it from their wheelchairs. If I carried on placing it to them I would lose the next game and the match.

I thought this harsh advice, it was only a game but I understood what she was trying to say. Game two got underway and it was me to serve first, before I was about to serve I glanced over at Olive and she gave me a reassuring nod in a Yoda like fashion from the film 'Star Wars.' I served to my opponent, he returned and I purposely tapped it over the net so he couldn't reach it from his wheelchair. I won two games to one and since

Madge

then I never look down on people with disabilities and treat them as my equal.

We returned to the youth club victorious, we didn't boast too much about the victory although it put us second in the league. We did let everyone know that Rigger was beaten not only by someone in a wheelchair but a woman to boot. He claimed he lost on purpose but to be honest she was good, I was glad I didn't have to play her.

There was always something to do at the Youth club, I feel sorry for kids today, those sort of clubs are on the decline.

The holidays were the best. We'd often go to the Lake District or Wales, mountain walking. Sheila was always in charge of any such ventures. She was in her mid forties and a hippy at heart. She had long scraggly brown hair, always in a ponytail and in the summer would always wear a black vest, she never shaved under her arms and the hairs would stick out from the vest, it was disgusting. She was a nice woman though and devoted a lot of time to kids.

The first mountain we were to walk was Mount Snowdon, the highest mountain in Wales. When I say 'walk,' there were parts that were quite scary and we would have to physically climb steep rock faces. It took about five and a half hours to reach the top and we were all knackered. I went along for a day out but never realised how hard it would be. I recall taking a well earned break half way up and sat thinking why am I doing this? When I could be lay in bed, what was the point? But I carried on and eventually we reached the top. The view was amazing, you could see for miles, I looked around and saw everybody's face. They all had that same look, rosy cheeks and a proud grin.

There's something quite satisfying about reaching the top of a mountain, a feeling of accomplishment. I'm not suggesting our exploits of walking Mount Snowdon were in the same bracket as Sir Edmund Hillary and Sherpa Tensing but this was our own little Everest.

We went on to walk and climb several mountains over the next few months, including Scafel Pyke, England's highest peak, situated in the Lake District.

The scariest we ever walked was Cader Idris in Wales. The walk itself went as normal, tough in parts and challenging but we eventually reached the top. Our guide was telling us how this particular mountain was reknowned for becoming invisible. He told us that from nowhere clouds would cover the peak and you wouldn't be able to see your hand in front of your face. In the event of this happening you would have to sit it out and wait for the clouds to lift. He said there have been a couple of occasions where walkers had fell over the edge to their death, trying to walk in the clouds. It was after one such incident that a stone hut had been built on the summit to encourage walkers to sit and wait. The hut was about twenty foot by ten foot with benches either side. It comfortably held about twenty people.

No sooner had he finished his well-rehearsed pep talk when the clouds started to thicken around us. We all looked at the guide, he told us to head for the hut. By the time we got to there you could barely see anything. Sheila did a head count, there was fifteen in the group but she could only count fourteen. Rigger, who else? Was missing. The youth leaders started to panic. They asked us when we last remembered seeing Rigger, we couldn't remember. The guide stood at the door of the hut shouting out to Rigger to stay put wherever he was and not attempt to walk anywhere. A couple of the girls in the group started crying, it was very eerie, here we were on top of a mountain, surrounded by clouds and one member of our group missing. What started out as a fun climb was turning out to be quite frightening.

We seemed to be in that cold little hut for an eternity, when in fact it was only about half an hour before the clouds lifted. The guide looked around but still couldn't find Rigger. We began descending the mountain, much quicker than normal and nobody spoke a word, the youth leaders and the guide had a look of sheer panic on their faces. The guide informed us that when we got to the bottom he would send a rescue team in search of Rigger.

We reached the bottom and a team of five men started getting kitted up quickly to go and find Rigger before nightfall. Sheila was in tears and was being reassured by the guide that everything would be fine and they would find Rigger safe and well.

We were told to go and wait in the small cafe and get something to eat. As we entered the cafe we were confronted with a familiar voice;

'You took your time didn't you? I've been here ages.' It was Rigger sat in the corner, eating a cheeseburger. It turns out, half way up the mountain he'd become tired and decided to walk back to the mini-bus and have a sleep. Had he informed someone it would have saved everyone being in a blind panic.

Sheila ran over and hugged him. Then her jubilation turned to anger and in her slightly posh accent said;

Madge

'You stupid little fucker, do you realise what you've caused? We thought you were dead.'

We'd never heard Sheila swear before and it sounded quite funny. Rigger obviously found it funny, his now trademark grin appeared on his face and he simply said; 'Soz.' Before taking another bite of his half eaten cheeseburger.

The event became part of youth club folklore and Sheila banned Rigger from any subsequent walks.

I'd been given a position of trust at the club, Ronnie, the youth club leader asked if I'd help out on Wednesdays with the juniors. It meant me missing Subbuteo night but I felt proud that he'd asked me, so I agreed. The position meant I could enter normally restricted areas, it felt good and I was even allowed to sit in on staff meetings on occasions. It wouldn't be long before I would abuse the trust shown in me.

At the other side of the youth club was a function room, which were the venue for wedding receptions most Friday and Saturdays. There was a small bar and they needed a barmaid. I used my position to get Madge a job. This was nothing like the Labour club, there was no late night drinking and she would be home for eleven pm at the latest.

On one Friday evening I did something I regret, even to this day. I'd left my mates at about ten-thirty and went to meet Madge at the club, she was working behind the bar. I parked my pushbike up against the wall and went into the bar, Madge informed me she would be about half an hour or so. As I was about to leave to wait outside, I noticed the office door was open and in it was sat Gina, she was a volunteer at the youth club and was three years older than me. She said I could wait in the office until Madge finished work. We sat chatting when she brought to my attention that the safe door was left open, I joked that we could take the money and no one would know it was us, there were hundreds of people there that night and anyone could have walked in. She then looked at me and said 'Go on then, half each.'

I laughed nervously but could see she was serious. She stood at the office door and told me to hurry up. I couldn't believe it, Gina was a well liked and a trusted volunteer. Without thinking I ran to the safe and took a bundle of money, I then went outside and inserted the cash inside the handlebars of my pushbike.

It wasn't long before Ronnie noticed the money had gone and he called the Police. The Police questioned everyone who had access to the office including Gina, they didn't give me a second thought, they weren't aware I'd even been in the office. When Madge and I arrived home, I went and put my bike in the shed and took the stolen money from inside the handlebars. There was £140, seventy pounds each for Gina and I. I secretly gave Gina her share the following day but I felt bad, not bad enough to give it back though. I told Madge that dad had given me some money as an early birthday present, they still didn't speak, so she'd never know.

I was now getting the taste for making easy money. I'd see less and less of Cal, Rigger and Brad and had started to hang about with Clive and his gang. He was impressed with my honesty over the fifty pence situation and told me every gang needs an honest member. There was Jimmy, he had the worst stutter I'd ever heard, then there was Ginger Lee, he was huge and finally Robbo, he was half-cast and originally came from Toxteth, a tough area in Liverpool. This gave me notoriety and the opportunity to make some money I was becoming accustomed to, albeit illegally. I was still attending the youth club but had quit the table tennis team and my position of trust, I felt I could no longer carry on as before, how could I?

This was also the time my sporadic school days were coming to an end. The final exams were approaching. I'd not done any revising so was unlikely to pass any of them with flying colours, with that in mind I decided not to take any at all, another decision I would later live to regret. Madge was furious, dad didn't really care and Donna told me I was stupid. I didn't listen to any of them, I knew better. I didn't even attend the last day of school, I was moving up in the world and making my own money... Who needed good exam results?

My Sixteenth birthday was approaching and I remember sitting in gran Karalius' house, my dad told me he was giving me one thousand pounds for my birthday and Christmas. I always hated that, my birthday is the 22nd of December, three days before Christmas and ever since I can remember people would buy me one 'big' present to cover both events. Dad had a big deal in the offing, he'd bought a load of stolen textiles and rented a warehouse just outside Widnes to house them. He was about to go to the warehouse with uncle Vin and Brian, I asked him could I go with them, he thought for a moment and told me not to tell Madge.

Dad had not long got out of prison for handling stolen goods but that never deterred him, he said nine to five jobs were for mugs and he'd show me how to make real money.

The thousand pounds never materialised, a guy called Manchester Joe had done a runner with all the ill-gotten gains and dad was left with nothing. My dads' life was a story of near misses. When he was twenty-one he was offered a contract to play for Widnes rugby league club, only to break his leg before setting foot on the pitch.

He then opened his own scrap yard, it was very successful and he made lots of money in the Sixties and early seventies, he would say it was like turning on a tap but instead of water coming out, it was money but like I mentioned earlier, dad liked the horses and no sooner had he made money, he'd gamble it away. He was half owner of a nightclub but didn't get on with his partner, instead of one buying the other out, they turned a card, dad drew a ten, his partner a queen. Dad lost half a nightclub on the turn of a card. I never got why he gambled, he wasn't very good at it.

His mates used to say he was an unlucky gambler, on one occasion he'd placed a five horse accumulator, the first four horses won and he stood to win £18,000 if the fifth one won. He and Vin were sat in the pub waiting for the last race when, apparently the bookie came in and offered to settle the bet there and then by giving dad £8,000 in cash. Dad refused and his last horse lost in a photo finish and he got nothing.

The most famous blunder that was told and retold several times over the years occurred whilst he was taking down an old clock tower in Winwick Hospital during the 1960's. An old lady approached my dad on the eve of the Grand National and asked would he place a bet on for her? She said she'd read the paper and saw one horse that trained with a goat, she used to have a goat in her earlier years and for that reason alone she wanted to put a pound on it to win. Dad agreed but when he saw the horse in the betting it was 100-1 and had no chance. So he'd tell the old lady he'd forgot to put the bet on and give her the one-pound back on Monday morning. The horse was called Foinavon and famously won the Grand National that year. It was coming last when all the other horses piled up at a fence enabling it to win the race. That fence was named after Foinavon and dad had to pay the old lady one hundred and one pounds the following Monday.

My dads' bad luck kept me away from gambling but I did inherit his illegal activities for a short time.

Clive had masterminded his latest venture, it again involved Ditton youth club. I was reluctant to further abuse the trust they'd shown me but by now was well and truly part of Clives' gang and had no choice but to go along. The plan was to make a hole in the fibreglass skylight situated on the roof of the Community Centre directly above where the beer was kept. We would then lower ropes into the room which had hooks on the bottom and simply lift the crates of beer out of the room. It all went like clockwork and we kept four crates for ourselves and sold the rest to an Off-licence who didn't care where it came from.

We stopped going to the youth club every night and found a new venue where we could hang out. At the top of Montgomery Road stood Sunnyside House, a huge three story white house. The front of the house was once a Barbers shop. It was known locally as 'Burkey's,' the guy who owned it was Eddie Burke, he was in his Sixties and to say he was eccentric would be putting it mildly, he was also bent as a ten bob note, as Madge used to say. He was over six foot tall with grey hair and always dressed immaculately and when he laughed his false teeth would fall out, that amused us every time. He would allow us to sit and drink beer in this huge house, it was also a good place to take girls. The neighbours hated him, because he was gay they thought he was a threat to their kids and the fact he was now letting teenagers use his house as a 'knocking shop' infuriated them even more. Looking back I think he was just lonely and even the company of rowdy teenagers was better than nothing.

It was in Eddie's house a gang of us sat down to watch Live Aid in 1985, we were having a party and Eddie was camping it up with the girls as usual when he disappeared. After twenty minutes or so he reappeared in a floral dress and badly put on make up. The party stopped and we all looked at him.

'What the fuck are you doin'?' Clive asked.

He held his hand out and there was blood everywhere, he'd slit his wrist with an old barbers razor. The girls started screaming and all hell broke loose. Eddie was taken away and eventually put into psychiatric care. The house was demolished some years later. Every time I hear 'Do they know its Christmas' by Band Aid, I see Eddie Burke, it's something that will unfortunately stay etched on my memory forever.

Our next venture was one too many, we'd been lucky so far but our luck was soon to run out. Clive had decided that computers were the future and that we should break into Widnes College and steal the computers, as his mum knew someone who'd buy them, no questions asked.

This was the biggest thing we'd ever done and had to be planned meticulously. It was September and the college was enrolling for the coming term, so I attended, pretending to be interested in Broadcasting and writing. (The irony wasn't lost on me either) In actual fact, I just wanted to see where they kept their computers.

The night arrived and we made our way to the college, Clive had got hold of some Walky-Talkies and we told Jimmy to climb up to the top of the Municipal buildings next door to the college and radio us if he saw any Police cars. The Police station was only five hundred yards from the college, this was perhaps our first mistake. Our biggest mistake of all was putting Jimmy as look out. Did I mention Jimmy had a bad stutter? We'd successfully got into the college, found our way to the computer room, when we were radioed by Jimmy;

'C-C-C-C-C-C-C.' He was trying to say something but by the time we could work out what, the Police had the college surrounded and we were arrested.

We got a £250 fine each and eighty hours community service. Madge threatened to throw me out the house if I carried on with my association with Clive. Aunty Bella was going to Towyn on holiday for a fortnight, Madge arranged for me to go with them. Some people thought my behaviour deserved punishment, not a holiday. This was punishment. I'd gone too far and was being banished.

As for breaking my association with Clive. That would be easier said than done, once you've played cards with the Devil, it's hard to get out of the game.

One thing was for sure, I had to do something, I was spiraling out of control and in danger of becoming like dad... A chip off the old block!

CHAPTER SEVEN

Summer Holidays.

I'd never felt so bad going on 'Holiday' before, there was a lot on my mind as we were traveling along Towyn sea front. I remember looking at all the sights, my head leaning on the rear passenger window and recalling the times I'd been here before, under happier circumstances.

Towyn and Rhyl in North Wales was and still is a popular holiday venue. Towyn is just like any other seaside resort the world over. The shops on the front littered with 'Kiss me quick' hats, burger stalls, and arcades with the odd pub for the adults. Everyone forgetting their troubles for a week or two.

We passed Happy Days Caravan Park, this was the camp where I spent my first holiday in Towyn in 1975, the year after gran Holland died.

I've touched upon Towyn in previous chapters but thought it would be appropriate to devote this chapter to the many holidays we spent there over the years, not one holiday went by without something of note taking place.

Aunty Bella and Madge decided to hire a caravan in Towyn in 1975, the previous year had been tough and a holiday would be a great tonic. There were seven of us in one eight birth caravan, Bella, Madge, Tony and his older brother Timmy, Donna and her friend Kay and of course myself. I was six years old and vaguely remember the excitement I felt about going on my first real holiday. Dad offered to run us to Towyn but there was too many of us to fit in his car, so we went by coach, or 'Charra' as they were known back then.

Donna, Kay and our Timmy were about the same age and didn't want to be hanging around with Tony and I. They were Thirteen and far too grown up to be seen with kids. Tony and I were quite happy playing football on the small field just behind our caravan. Tony was in goal and I was taking penalties at him, when a voice from nowhere;

'Put yer foot over the ball.' He said with a soft Scottish accent, he then took the ball off me and placed it on the penalty spot.

'Like this.' He said.

He placed the ball in the bottom left hand corner, sending Tony the wrong way.

'That's how it's done laddie.' He added with a wink. He was only a small man with curly ginger hair. He went on to tell us his name;

'Billy Bremner boys, pleased to meet ya.'

Bily Bremner was a prominant footballer in the Seventies and played for Leeds United in their glory years, he stayed for about ten minutes and left.

We picked up our ball and ran to the caravan to tell Madge and Bella who we'd just met, they were not impressed and I don't think they quite believed us.

'What would Billy Bremner be doing on Happy Days Caravan Park?' Asked Bella.

'Hardly George Best.' Madge quipped.

I'm not sure if we really did meet Billy Bremner that day, or someone pretending to be him. Regardless, when we got home we told all our mates whom we'd met on holiday. They were all Liverpool, Everton or Man United fans and as a result were even less impressed than Madge and Bella. To make the story more incredible we changed a few things over the years and told people we'd met Kevin Keegan instead, that got their attention. We even got uncle Archie to sign a ball in Keegans' style. We told the story that many times, we convinced ourselves that we'd met the great man himself that beautiful sunny day in Towyn.

This was the same holiday when the saying 'Take the Bull by the Horns' took a literal meaning. We were all sat playing cards in the caravan, waiting for tea to be cooked when our Timmy let out an uncharacteristic girlie scream, we all turned around and looked in the same direction as he was looking, there was a bulls head peeking in the doorway of the caravan, it was huge. We all started screaming and tried to run for cover, that in itself was easier said than done, the caravan was only small. Madge and Bella, to my amazement, ran over to the bull, grabbed a horn each and tried to push it backwards out of the caravan. The bull was pushing back and winning, it was entering the caravan. It was a terrifying event but out of nowhere Timmy picked up a pan off the small cooker, ran up to the bull and hit it square in the head. We all stood like statues waiting to see the bulls reaction, no one said a word... the bull seemed to look at Timmy as if to say 'That hurt,' and quietly backed out of the caravan and headed off down the road. With each caravan the bull approached all you could hear was screams and doors being slammed shut.

The bull was eventually caught and no harm was done, except to our Timmys' street cred for letting out 'That' scream. He never lived it down.

We returned to Towyn two years later. We stayed on Wyncups Caravan Park this time, it was a better camp. There was a lot more of us, Aunty Fiona and Uncle Paul had decided to come along with their daughter Sam, who was around Donnas' age. Madge still hadn't totally forgiven her for what happened at grans' house after she died but she made the effort. Madge would spend most of the day in the small bingo on the camp. Everyday she would come back to the caravan with fist fulls of tokens she'd won. Instead of winning prizes, you'd be handed tokens for each line you won, you needed about twenty of these tokens to collect one crappy prize. Usually the prizes were Welsh Dolls or cheap Teddy Bears, not even good enough to palm off on somebody as a present when you got home, it did work out to my advantage, one of the prizes was a big bag of soldiers. Again they were cheap and nasty and not to the 'Hobby Shop' standard I was accustomed to but they could join my army of over 500, if only as sacrificial lambs, they would always die first. They would also be the ones that I would cut off their arms or legs and daub with red paint to give the affect of blood. They had a tough existence... but this was war and sacrifices had to be made.

This was also the year the world was rocked by the loss of one of its best loved sons.

We were in Wyncups club enjoying the nights' entertainment. I use the word entertainment very loosely. Anyone who's ever been to one of these clubs will know what I mean. The customary talent show, parents would tell their kids they could actually sing and encourage them to get up on stage and humiliate themselves. Do I sound bitter? I am, I was one of those kids. I'm not bitter because I was persuaded to get up on stage and strut my stuff but I come third to a 'Nolan Sisters' tribute act and a fat kid dressed as the Honey Monster, it was a fix. My rendition of *Everybody was Kung-Fu-Fighting* should have won hands down. How can two girls and

Madge

a boy, albeit, a very feminine boy, win a talent show as The Nolan Sisters. It scarred me for... a couple of minutes anyway.

My mood was soon lifted. Madge won £80 on the bandit and she gave us all five pounds each. We went to the arcade next door and had a great time. I won a small Koala bear soft toy on the grab machine, it cost me about three pounds to win it. I could have bought the same toy for one pound in the shop next door but where's the challenge in that. I ran back to the club to give Madge her present but something had happened. People were hugging each other and crying, even grown men. Madge ran up to me and sat me down;

'Andrew.' She said, in tears. 'He's dead.' 'My dad?' I asked.

'No son, Elvis, the King is dead.'

Who the fuck was Elvis, I was only Eight years old and didn't understand any of what was going on and I was quite confused because I was sure we had a Queen. In fact I know we had a queen, we'd queued up for three hours on Kingsway outside Simms Cross school just weeks previous. Three hours holding a plastic Union Jack on a stick. I didn't even get to see her face, she had her head turned.

The night went on but it was more like a wake than a party. I never quite understood the impact one mans' death could have on so many people. For the rest of the holiday, every-time one of us would become a bit rowdy, one of the adults would remind us;

'Behave, Elvis is dead!'

His death did have an affect on me personally... he ruined my holiday!

Despite the tackiness of seaside holidays, I've always enjoyed them. Apart from the Towyn holidays I'm relaying, I've been to numerous resorts all over the country, my favourite is Illfracombe, North Devon. It's nothing like Towyn, it almost apologises for being a tourist trap. On my first visit with my wife and kids, I felt like I was intruding on this beautiful small town but the fact is, they need tourists' money to survive. It was here that whilst I was ordering a Devon cream tea for my wife and I. I noticed on the television in the background two tall buildings on fire. I asked the man serving what was going on. He told me two planes had crashed into the World Trade Centre in New York. Unlike the Elvis incident, I knew full well the implications of this shocking event. Not only do these things occur when I'm on holiday but 9/11 also happens to be my wedding anniversary. Maybe it's me... maybe I'm a jinx! The reason I'm interrupting with this more current event is because after nine eleven, for the rest of the holiday, every time one of the kids would play up a bit, my wife and I would turn to them and say;

'Behave, people in New York have died!'

We went back to Towyn the following year, it was 1978. Elvis fever was still gripping the world, though now it was more celebratory and you didn't have to feel guilty for wanting to enjoy yourself. The usual suspects were going, except Aunty Fiona. I'd knocked Uncle Paul on his arse the previous Winter with a snowball, when Fiona was bouncing over the road to tell Madge what I'd done I threw a snowball at her causing her to slip and sprain her ankle. Her and Madge fell out over it and still weren't speaking.

Madge allowed dad to take us on this occasion. He pulled up outside the house in a racing green Jaguar, it was a beautiful car and we felt like millionaires arriving in Towyn. The holiday was going well and nothing of note had taken place, that was about to change.

It turns out that gran Karalius was on a neighbouring caravan site with aunty Mavis and her five sons. Gran always liked Madge, she felt sorry for her, the way dad had treated her over the years. She apparently was with Madge some years previously when dad was in the pub and Madge needed money for food for Donna, who was still a baby. Women didn't go in pubs in those days, so Madge waited for over an hour with gran Karalius outside. Dad finally came out with an envelope full of money. When they got back to grans' and opened it. I was full of newspaper cut to the size of money. Gran Karalius was ashamed of her son.

Yes, I think there was a mutual respect between gran and Madge and even though they'd not seen each other for some time, they agreed to meet up for a game of bingo in the Black Cat. The Black Cat was a huge bingo and arcade on Towyns' main road. I recall playing on the bumper cars with my cousin Brendan, Mavis's second eldest son and our Tony, when people started screaming and running for the exit. A fire had broken out in the slot machine area. This should have been filmed and used by the fire brigade as an example how not to react in the event of a fire. Sheer panic, the exit doors were becoming blocked, there were some people jumping through glass windows to escape.

The bingo caller was trying to tell everyone to calm down and commended gran Karalius for staying cool. Gran was deaf as a post and didn't even realise the chaos behind her;

'What did you say?' Gran said to the bingo caller.

'Well done missus for stayin' calm.' He replied.

'Why wouldn't I be calm?' She replied, with that she looked around and saw the fire;

'Shite.' She screamed and ran for the exit. She was in her seventies but was pushing grown men out of the way.

The following day the Black Cat was almost reduced to the ground and the firemen were still dousing the hot ashes.

For days after, kids, including myself were rummaging through the debris looking for coins and anything we could salvage for personal gain. Miraculously, no one was killed in the fire that night.

The holiday was coming to an end. It was the last night and we went to the club for the end of holiday finale. The talent contest was the main event, I was once bitten, twice shy and had no intention of humiliating myself like I did previously but there were plenty in our group that would.

Gran and Madge urged Brendan to take part. He got on stage and sang *'Do Ya Wanna' be in my gang'?* By Gary Glitter. Brendan only knew the chorus and sang it for nearly ten minutes, the compere tried several times to stop him but Brendan was in full swing and wouldn't budge. Someone finally turned off the sound system and gave Brendan a bag of soldiers to get him off stage. Brendan thought this was a prize and that he'd won the contest, nobody had the heart to tell him any different. The fact that Brendan thought he'd won encouraged him to enter another talent contest the following year. Donna had to wear a tube bandage on her leg due to an earlier operation to remove some cartilage from her right knee. She put one of the bandages over Brendans' head and put a trilby on him. He entered the contest as the invisible man. He had to be guided on stage because Donna had neglected to put eye holes in the bandage. It was quite funny, I recall the compere announcing Brendan on stage.

'Our next contestant is Brendan from Widnes. He's entered as the invisible man… only problem is we can't find him.'

Brendan actually came second and his stint as the invisible man went down in family history.

Morning arrived and it was time to pack, this was the worst thing about holidays, coming home. Dad was due to come and pick us up, he turned up in an old pick-up van, Madge was mortified;

'Where's the Jag?' She asked.

Dad said it was in the garage for repairs, in fact, it turns out he'd lost it in a card game. So the pick-up would have to do. There wasn't enough room for all of us, so Donna went home with Mavis and Tony and I had to sit in the back of the pick-up all the way back to Widnes. We loved it, it was exciting. In truth we'd been let down again by dad.

I went to Towyn recently and was sad to see how much disrepair it was now in, maybe it always was and I was simply seeing it back then through a childs' eyes. Either way they were good memories but memories are things of the past and I had face what lay ahead of me back home, in Ditton.

My latest Towyn holiday was also coming to an end, I didn't enjoy it much. I was constantly reminded why I was there. I knew I had to go home. I knew I'd let Madge down with my criminal activities. Most of all I had to tell Clive I was leaving his gang, there was bound to be repercussions and not good ones.

Aunty Bella dropped me off at Parbold Court. I got my bag out of the boot and watched the car drive away. I felt alone and scared, I walked up the path, Madge opened the door and I stopped half way;

'Are we alright mum?' I asked.

She walked down the path and took my bag. She then kissed me on the cheek and said;

'We will be son.'

Just like gran Karalius, no matter what your children do, you always blame yourself for their mistakes. You love them and ultimately forgive them. Despite what everyone said about me going on 'holiday' as a punishment, Madge pulled off a masterstroke. It certainly had the desired affect, as I was about to put my criminal activities behind me once and for all.

CHAPTER EIGHT

REDEMPTION.

I had one weekend left before I was due to start my Community service. I should have enjoyed the freedom but I didn't move out of the house. I knew Clive was in waiting, I'd heard it on the grapevine that he wanted a 'word.' I don't mind admitting I was shitting myself.

As I sat watching Columbo on a dull Friday afternoon, there was a knock on the door. I pulled the net curtain back to see who it was, it was Clive. I wasn't going to answer but he'd already seen me.

I reluctantly opened the door, he stood combing his Afro and with a wink, he said;

'Not seen ya for a couple of weeks, are you avoiding me?'

I explained to him I'd been on holiday. I then told him that I wouldn't be hanging around with him anymore. His facial expression turned menacing, I told him I'd be thrown out of the house if I didn't break ties. He put his Afro comb in his back pocket and asked;

'Is it because I'm black? Is your mam a racist?'

That notion was absurd, Madge liked Clive at first but she did blame him for my criminal activities. In truth, they'd started long before I met him. Clive enjoyed intimidating people and he knew I was scared, he winked at me again and said with malice in his voice;

'See ya' soon Andy lad, really soon.' He walked down the path with his customary swagger.

I shut the door, my stomach was turning, I knew he meant what he said and I would indeed be seeing him soon. I sat back down and carried on watching Columbo, trying to take my mind away from what just happened. Columbo was one of Madge's favourite programmes. She loved the way he used to catch the murderer. She once joked that if he ever walked up our path, she'd give herself up immediately, if she'd done anything or not. Her love affair with the fictional detective was about to come to an abrupt end.

For those who have never seen Columbo before, let me enlighten you. Every episode had a famous guest star, who became the murderer and would ultimately be caught by the disheveled Columbo. One particular episode the producers made the fatal mistake of casting Johnny Cash as the villain. Madge loved Columbo but adored Johnny Cash, when Columbo arrested her hero, they lost Madge's loyal viewing forever. She refused to watch the programme again. I reminded her several times it wasn't real it was just a television programme but Madge never forgave him.

The rest of the weekend passed without much event. I sat in the living room on a miserable rainy Sunday afternoon with the curtains half shut, the room was dreary and grey, it matched my mood. Then to make things worse, 'The Last of The Summer Wine' came on the television, I hate that programme, along with 'The Antiques Roadshow.' Not because of the programmes themselves but because they epitomised Sundays. Gran Holland used to say Sundays were clock watching days, everyone used to watch time slip away on Sunday, knowing their humdrum week was approaching with each passing minute.

'Sunday again.' She'd say. 'One week closer to the knackers yard.' Optimism wasn't one of her virtues. She did have a love of the English language. I attribute my love of writing and words to her. She had many ponderous questions and would say to people, things like;

'Why are Sundays so called... when it always rains?' 'Why is the word BIG... so small?'

'Why does the word funeral start with the word... fun?'

She also bought me an Andy Capp paperback annual, which initiated my love of drawing and reading cartoon strips. It still stands pride of place in my small book collection.

Monday morning came around too quickly. It was time to repay my debt to society in the form of Community service. Unlike my first day of secondary school, no one was waving me off with a proud grin across their faces. I'd brought shame on Madge, she never said that but I knew, I could see it in her face. It was a bus ride away but I decided to leave early and take a slow walk, I wasn't looking forward to it one bit. I did contemplate bunking off but this wasn't school, the consequences would have been severe.

I wasn't quite sure where to go, I knew which building it was but it was a big building. It had many different offices, different companies. All I knew it was called Legal House Building. I thought this ironic, given the fact practically everyone there had done something illegal. I didn't have to look very hard for where I had to go. Outside one particular fire door stood four young lads, about my age, wearing bright yellow high viz jackets and baseball caps. Each smoking a disjointed cigarette. Yes, this was definitely the place. At least Clive wasn't there. Because of my imposed holiday, he was already two weeks into his community service.

I approached the lads and asked them if this was the place you came for community service, they stopped talking and all stared at me, I say all, one of the lads had a turn in his eye and I wasn't quite sure if he was looking at me or not. He must have sensed I was looking at him in particular and he snapped;

'Got a f-f-fucking problem l-l-lad?' This poor bastard must have been dropped on his head as a kid, I thought. Before I could answer a voice came from inside summoning us to go in. The lads took one last prolonged drag of their cigarette, threw them to the ground and we all went inside.

We were told to take a seat by a man in his early forties. He was well groomed, shirt and tie and was very much trying to 'get down with the kids.'

'Back with us again Tommy.' He said to the lad with the turn in his eye. He'd obviously been here before and not learned a thing. We were informed that we would be taken to Victoria Park to clean up litter left over from the previous weekends Vintage car rally. A big burly guy then entered the room and threw me a high viz jacket, he was an ex-con come good and had worked his way up to become a volunteer at the community service centre. A clever piece of PR on there part, it showed that if he could turn his life around, anyone could. His name was Steve and he would be our supervisor for the day, it was clear he would not be taking any shit off a bunch of cocky teenagers.

'Come on Tommy, you know the drill by now lad, get in the van.' Steve said.

Tommy actually looked proud to be singled out, a smug grin appeared on his face. We arrived at Victoria Park, it was a freezing October morning and the place was in a right mess. There were only five of us, it was going to take all day. Two hours in I picked up a piece of paper and found a wallet, I looked around to see if anyone had seen it, they hadn't. I opened the wallet and found thirty pounds and a bank card with a mans name on it. I struggled about what to do, should I put it in my pocket and not say anything, or do the decent thing and give it to Steve. I did nothing for a while, the fact I was even thinking of handing it in meant I was getting somewhere. A week ago I would have took the money and ditched the wallet.

Our time was up and we'd worked hard, I told myself that if I kept the money, it would be like a days wage for a job well done.

I never said anything to Steve and kept the wallet in my pocket. It was when I was walking home that it hit me... I felt bad. I'd promised myself and Madge that I was going to change. Alright, I didn't steal the wallet but I didn't earn it either. I stopped in my tracks, turned around and walked to the Police Station. Standing outside, I thought about it again, thirty pounds would come in really handy, it would help Madge out and I'd just say I got it from dad, like I usually did. Without another thought I walked quickly into the police station, before I could change my mind and handed it in. The desk sergeant took my name and address and congratulated me on 'Doing the right thing.' Walking home that day I felt good in myself, for the first time in a long time, I felt clean.

I never told Madge what happened, I didn't have to. Two days later there was a knock on our front door, Madge answered it. I heard her invite someone in, it was a man and his wife, he was the owner of the wallet. He thanked me for handing the wallet in and handed me a twenty-pound note, I told him I didn't do it for the money but he insisted. His wife went on to tell Madge that in the wallet was not only money, which can be replaced, or the bank-card, which can be cancelled but there was a scan photo of their baby, whom she miscarried at seven months pregnant and that one photo was all they had to remember their baby by.

They thanked me again and left. Madge hugged me and told me how proud she was of me. That wallet probably changed my life, where would I be if I'd kept it? I believe fate led me to find that wallet that freezing morning at Victoria Park... a test.

Still feeling full of pride, I decided the next day to go to the youth club and offer my services as a volunteer. They never knew it was me who took the money from the safe or stole the beer. I saw this as a chance to redeem myself, give something back to the youth club. I got half way there and decided to take a short cut through the derelict garages. From behind the

Madge

second garage I heard a noise, I looked back to see what it was, I couldn't see anything. I turned back and there stood Clive, Robbo and Jimmy;

'Alright Andy lad.' Clive said.

I knew this wasn't going to be good, I went to turn back but Lee stood in front of me. I was outnumbered but that was the way Clive was, he liked the odds to be in his favour. My dads voice came into my head;

'If you're going to go down... take one of them with you.'

I saw Clive take his right hand out of his pocket, before he could move I punched him square in the jaw, he stumbled backwards, rubbed his face and said;

'That's what I liked about you... you had balls.'

The four of them started kicking seven kinds of shite out of me, they stopped after about five minutes, then stood me up;

'Is that it? Are we quits?' I asked, wiping away the blood from my face.

'We h-had to do it Andy.' Said Jimmy.

I knew that, you didn't leave Clives' gang without paying a price. I think he liked me and didn't want to beat me up but he had a reputation to uphold. I'd never been beat up before or after so apologetically.

I limped back to the house to clean myself up, I was in agony but the pain wasn't as bad as the anticipation. I was just glad it was all over.

The next morning brought good news for a change. My acceptance came through the post, I got a place on a YTS course doing bricklaying and was due to start in two weeks. I told Madge and she said we'd go and have a celebratory lunch with the twenty-pounds reward I got for handing in the wallet. We hopped on the bus and went to the Town centre, we went to the Rendezvous cafe. Ever since I was a kid we'd been going there. We used to meet aunty Bella there three times a week when we lived in Sinclair, Madge and Bella would sit talking for hours, I would always have my favourite meal, chips, pasty and gravy, followed by an egg custard. We stopped going when the owner Tom sold up, he never had a choice in selling. Tom was about six foot with a mop of black hair and a beard. At weekends he stayed at his caravan on the Yorkshire moors. This was about the time the Yorkshire Ripper was at large, because of Toms' appearance and his links with Yorkshire he was arrested twice in connection with the murders. He was innocent but people thought there was no smoke without fire and he was hounded out of the town, the word pervert was even painted across the window of the cafe.

It was in the Rendezvous that I would sit as a child and look at the human condition. Because we were there for a while, the turn over of people was frequent. I would imagine what the different characters lives would be like and make up stories in my head about them. The regulars had their own seats, they would buy the same meal every day. Mr Hopkins would sit by the window between eleven and eleven-thirty every Monday and Wednesday morning. He always ordered a plain ham sandwich with no butter and a cup of tea without any milk. I don't know if that was his name but that's what I called him. I imagined him to live alone, a creature of habit. He would probably be a train-spotter or collect stamps. He always wore a shirt and tie but the shirt was always soiled around the collars. I got all this information in my head just by the sandwich he ordered. I think you can tell a lot about a person by the sandwich they eat. Plain ham with no butter… trains, stamps. Definitely! One particular day Madge, Bella and I were sat at our usual table when a man walked in. He was unshaven, tatty looking with a bag under his arm. He then sat at the table opposite us with just a plate of peas and a cup of tea. It was obvious he had no money. Madge leaned over and whispered to him;

'I'm not being funny love but would you like some chips with that?'

The man gratefully accepted and told Madge he'd just been released from prison. Always a sucker for a sob story, Madge and Bella clubbed enough together for ten cigarettes for him. He thanked them and left. We went back to the cafe the following day. After being there for half an hour the man from the previous day walked in again. He sat across from us and said;

'Are ya' getting' the chips in love?'

Madge was shocked but bought him some chips anyway. She avoided the cafe for a week afterwards, instead of just telling him straight. That was Madge in a nutshell, she would give people her last penny, probably why she never had anything herself.

The cafe wasn't quite the same as it was back then, when Tom owned it, maybe because I was older. I was three months away from my seventeenth birthday and about to start my working life. I was excited and scared at the same time. There was the little matter of my community service to finish before I could start the YTS course, to finish as quickly as possible I went every day for the next week. On my final day, I realised why Steve was doing this work as a volunteer. We were sent to do some painting at the Ethel Hanley care home for the elderly. I was busy glossing the skirting boards in the corridor when I noticed Steve going into one of the resident's rooms. I never gave it much thought, until later that day we were all

Madge

gathered together and told the police wanted to talk to us. Some expensive jewellery had gone missing from a residents' room. The same room I saw Steve enter earlier, I never told anyone, what would be the point? Steve was their success story and we were there repaying our debt to society, of course it must have been one of us. The police came and questioned us but they never got to the bottom of it. I knew who did it though and I think Steve knew I knew, he couldn't look me in the eye. One of the other lads said this wasn't the first time things had gone missing, Steve the ex-con hadn't 'come good' after all. I was glad I never handed him that wallet. That also would have mysteriously disappeared.

I was starting to repay my debts. I'd finished my community service and started to do some voluntary work at the Youth club. Ronnie had gone on to pastures new. His replacement Brian was a great guy and welcomed me back into the fold with open arms. We were due to go on a weekend trip to the Lake District. I went home on the Friday evening but had forgot my key. Madge was at Maggie's house, I went over to get her key. What happened next will stay in my memory forever. Madge had one sherry too many and was asleep in the chair, Maggie was still drinking and told me to take a seat, we sat chatting for a while, it was approaching midnight and all her kids were asleep. The younger two were on the settee covered with bath towels. Maggie then told me she missed having a man around the house, she then told me the leg on her bed was broke and she couldn't fix it. I innocently offered to fix it for her. I was thinking when I got back from the Lakes. Maggie thanked me and staggered upstairs, indicating for me to follow. Still not suspecting anything, I followed. We went into her bedroom and I immediately went to the bed. I lay on my back with my head under the bed, it was broken but could be easily fixed, a screw had come out. As I started to put the screw back in I felt the zip on my jeans started to open, I wandered what was happening. I came from under the bed and saw Maggie with her hand down my pants;

'What are you doing?' I asked.

She put her finger over her lips, as if to say 'be quiet,' I shit myself. Maggie was not the type of woman to take no for an answer. Her head started to lean towards my groin when Madge opened the bedroom door;

'What the hell is going on here?' She shouted.

I jumped up and ran past Madge and out of the house, I stayed in the shed that night. I was due to leave for the Lakes at eight O'clock the next morning, so I had to get in the house to get my stuff. It was freezing in the shed and I couldn't get any sleep. It was then I noticed the upstairs toilet window was slightly open. I scrambled up the drainpipe, making as little noise as I could, I finally got to the window and started to climb through it, then from nowhere, I heard someone in the back garden... it was the police, a neighbour must have phoned them, thinking I was a burglar. They told me to come down. It took me over an hour to get up there, I scrambled back down the drainpipe and told them I lived there, they immediately put me in handcuffs and told me I was under arrest. Again I told them that this was my house. They knocked on the door but could get no answer, Madge was well out of it, an earthquake wouldn't have woke her up. This added more credibility to me being a cat burglar... the house was empty and given the fact it was nearly three O'clock in the morning, even I could see how it looked. So for all my recent efforts I found myself back in the police cells. It was only at eight-thirty the next morning, when the desk sergeant came on duty that they checked my name, they then looked at my previous and found my file address was the one I'd supposedly been trying to break into. To be fair the sergeant was alright, I explained I was suppose to be going away with the Youth club half an hour ago and he arranged for me to get a lift home.

I still couldn't wake Madge, so I had to do the drainpipe thing all over again, I finally got into the house. I got all my stuff and ran to the Youth club. It was nearly nine O'clock, they'd long left. I put my bag on the floor and sat there for a while. I looked at the row of houses in front of me and wondered what their lives were like? Would they consider swapping with mine, I laughed to myself... not a chance. I took out one of my sandwiches that I prepared the day before and sat on the Youth club steps eating merrily away at my Jam and Peanut butter butty. I looked over to the playing fields and saw a small boy playing football with his dad. I felt slightly jealous of the boy, not so much because he was playing football with his dad but because his football kit matched, Everton top, Everton shorts and Everton socks... Everything matched, just like it should.

I got up and walked slowly home, I felt bad because once again I'd let the club down. I can honestly say the chain of events the previous evening, for once, was not my fault. I bumped into Clive on the way home, I hoped he wasn't going to give me another beating, that would really have rounded my day off, he just looked in my direction and put his hand up. I did likewise. He told me some time later what I already suspected. The beating wasn't personal... It was just business.

I finally got into the house and explained to Madge what happened at Maggie's house the night before. Like always, she didn't want to talk about it. I in turn explained to Brian what happened when they got back from the Lakes on Monday evening, he understood and found it all quite funny, I found it anything but. No matter how hard I was trying, doing things by the book was hard work but I was determined to carry on.

Madge's drinking was again becoming erratic. This sort of drinking was usually brought on by an event of some sort. It was clear what was irking her this time, Donna's impending wedding!

I was quite looking forward to it, I liked a good wedding, particularly the nighttime. There was always girls there and I'd just had the back of my hair permed and grew a few hairs above my lip... I was a babe magnet, how could I fail.

I had my YTS course to attend before I could think about the wedding. I was about to become a Bricklayer. It wouldn't take me long to qualify I thought and I would go on to own my own building firm and live happily ever after...I had to have dreams, what else is there. What I didn't realise was going on a bricklaying course meant I would end up working in pubs cleaning pool tables.

My first day on the course was filling out paperwork, I made some new friends. Rigger was on the course and we resumed our friendship, not to the degree we used to. Our Subbuteo days had well and truly gone. He told me Brad had started smoking pot and Cal was engaged to be married, he was only sixteen but that's how he was, the first girl he ever kissed would always be the love of his life. He was a good lad and I wished him well. He went on to marry and had three kids by the time he was Twenty-one and was divorced at Twenty-two, too much too young? Maybe.

I picked up my first wage on the Friday afternoon. Twenty-Seven pounds and Thirty Pence, Ten pounds a week keep to Madge, I had Seventeen quid a week all to myself... I was loaded!

The course itself started off well, we learnt the basic skills of bricklaying. We'd spend all day building walls, instead of using sand and cement we would use sand and water. It made sense, after we built a wall, it could be easily knocked down again. After two weeks we were sent on placement or work experience. Rigger and I were sent to BJ Fencing. It was hard work, we started at eight in the morning and finished at six at night. I didn't mind hard work but this was slave labour, the lads we were working alongside were on £200 a week and we were on £27.30. I went back to St Marie's old school building (the base for the YTS scheme) and told the head of the course that I'd come here to learn bricklaying, not to mix concrete for ten hours a day. He took me off the placement and I was again building walls, to knock back down again.

It did have its advantages. Riggers uncle wanted a garden wall building, we said we'd do it for Fifty pounds. We started on the Saturday morning and worked until about three O'clock. The wall looked really good, our training was paying off. We were due to go back the next day to finish off and collect our money. We went back bright and early Sunday morning and to our horror the wall we'd spent all day building had fell over, his uncle came out and asked how deep were the footings we'd put in. Rigger looked at me in bemusement, then back at his uncle and said;

'What are footings?'

What a pair of dickheads, we'd built the perfect wall but neglected to lay any foundations. That was the end of that, his uncle got someone else in to do the job. We never mentioned it to anyone at the YTS on the Monday morning. The least said the better.

I was called in to see the head tutor, he told me he had another placement for me, I told him I wouldn't be doing any slave labour again and declined his offer and got up to walk out.

'That's a shame.' He said 'This is working for a Pool and Snooker company, on St Michaels industrial estate in Ditton.'

He'd got my attention, Pool... Snooker... St Michaels, a two-minute walk from my house, tell me more! This placement also had nothing to do with bricklaying either but I was very selective with which jobs I would complain about. I arrived on my first day and was met by the owner. He was an Asian guy and wore a black Turban, his name was Ali. I was told the job entailed traveling around the North West with another guy, cleaning Pool tables they rented out, mainly to pubs and clubs. John Gillbanks was the other guy and was due in within the hour. John was a scouser and of course was known as 'Gilly.' Ali told me to go and have a game of pool on the table in the back while I waited for Gilly. This was the best job I've ever had.

Gilly would drive, he was an ex-professional footballer and used to play for Rochdale. We travelled all over, cleaning and servicing pool tables. One day we went to Wrexham football ground to empty the money from the table, when we got there the table was full and the barmaid said they had to take the money behind the bar. She handed Gilly £142 in fifty pence pieces. His eyes lit up. When we got in the van, he split the money between us, saying that Ali would be happy with the takings that were in the table. I wasn't going to argue and I didn't see it as stealing, it was given to me.

Madge

Another time we went to a pub in Toxteth, a tough Liverpool suburb, predominately inhabited by coloured people. It was the scene of violent riots in the 1980's and a place you wouldn't go, unless invited. Gilly assured me we'd be fine, the pub we were going to was owned by 'Big Eddie,' he was an Afro-Caribbean and stood nearly seven foot tall. Eddie was about Sixty years of age but was still revered in the neighbourhood. We got some funny looks when we pulled up outside the pub but to my relief Eddie came out to meet us. He shouted over to a gang of coloured youths stood on the corner;

'These guys are my guests... so this van will be safe here, RIGHT?'

They all nodded in acknowledgment. I got to work, ironing the tablecloth, Gilly stood at the bar with Eddie and had a pint. I then had to trim the cloth, I asked Gilly did he have a knife. Out of nowhere a coloured guy produced a six inch blade from inside his jacket... my face must have been a picture, after a couple of seconds of quiet, Eddie, Gilly and the coloured guy broke out into laughter. Eddie offered me a pint, I needed it.

It was odd, the rougher the area, the more hospitable they seemed to be. We went to a golf club in Lytham St Anne's near Blackpool, they had money and wanted us in and out as quickly as possible, we were in their way, the hired help.

I was given the keys to the unit one night, so I could open up in the morning, I stayed there until ten O'clock playing pool in the back, I even invited my mates over, it was a great job, until I got there one morning and the place was locked up, Gilly turned up and told me Ali had gone back down south. It turns out he had many little businesses like this one. He used them to launder money, he'd keep them open for about three months then disappear.

It was back to the YTS base for me, I missed that job, if you could call it that. The bricklaying was going well, we would stay in the base all week then when we got paid on a Friday we would go to the Market pub and have a few pints, the owner knew we were under-age but didn't seem to care. Looking back I think my drinking was starting to get out of hand and would only get worse. I did stay away from illegal activity though. I did voluntary work at the Youth club, as well as my daytime job. I think I was getting somewhere and finally getting some redemption.

CHAPTER NINE

BACK TO SCHOOL.

Donna's wedding was five days away. Madge was drinking more. She was becoming more agitated with each passing day. I couldn't understand why she was so against the wedding. Peter was alright and Donna seemed to be happy. That should have been enough but with Madge, it never was.

The night before the wedding she'd been at Maggie's house. She could vent all her anger to Maggie and she would agree with Madge, she didn't care. She would have agreed with Hitler if he'd brought a bottle of sherry with him.

The day of the wedding finally arrived. Madge told me she wasn't going. I persuaded her to change her mind. Donna had arranged for us to be picked up by one of Peter's relatives. This didn't sit pretty with Madge, she wanted to be in the main car. To be honest I think she was looking for any excuse not to go. We finally arrived at Runcorn Registry Office, all the Karalius clan was there, you could cut the atmosphere with a knife. I recently looked back at some photos of the wedding, there was one of Madge and dad stood either side of Donna, Madge didn't look happy. She'd made the effort and had her hair done and wore a two-piece navy blue suit that Donna had bought her for the wedding.

The day went off without event. Donna looked beautiful. The only down side was the snow, it was a winter wedding and the snow was two inches thick. The damp weather was playing havoc with my freshly permed mullet. I would have to re-mousse it before the night time if I was going to pull myself a stunner, no girl worth her salt would fancy a lad with a frizzy perm.

We all came back to Widnes and went to a local Social Club, it wasn't a bad day but I was saving myself for the night, so I only had one pint.

Madge never drank either, despite her problems with drink, she would confine it to behind closed doors. I think she knew what she was like when she had one too many and given everything, she never wanted to ruin Donna's day... not in that way.

Because of the burglaries in Ditton and the fact we'd already been robbed once, Madge had arranged with our next door neighbours to borrow their Alsatian dog to sit in our house while we were out, Duke went and stayed at Maggie's. The Alsatian was locked in the house and Madge was stood outside waiting for a lift to the party on the night, I was already there. This is where things started to go a bit pear-shaped.

Madge waited for half an hour for her lift. Peter's relative had got a flat tyre and couldn't pick her up. That was the excuse she needed, she went back in the house to try and get in touch with Donna, to tell her she wouldn't be going the wedding.

She stood in the hallway on the phone when she heard a noise behind her. She'd forgot all about next doors Alsatian being in the house, he stood there growling at Madge;

'Sit down Bruno... good dog, it's me... this is my house....' Madge said, doing her best Barbara Woodhouse impersonation.

Bruno growled more aggressively, showing his sharp fangs. She dropped the phone and ran down the hallway, slamming the door shut behind her. The neighbours who lent her the dog were out for the evening. In contrast to Duke, Bruno was a good guard dog, so good, he wouldn't let Madge into her own house.

Madge went to Maggie's house and never went to Donna's wedding reception on the evening. I don't think Donna forgave her for that, to be fair, it wasn't really Madge's fault but you couldn't blame Donna for thinking it was done purposely.

My evening was going quite well, the room was jam packed and there were plenty of girls there. I had my sights set on one in particular, she was a friend of one of Peter's relatives. I waited until the end of the night and asked her did she want to do a 'slowy.' She agreed, my perm was knocking the girls dead. I'd over-indulged with too much food and drink and was starting to feel a bit sick. We were dancing to *Just my imagination*, by The Temptations with her head on my shoulder. It was very romantic, she went to kiss me, with that I felt the nights lager resurfacing. I moved my head to one side and threw up over uncle Vin's back. The girl looked me up and down in disgust and walked away.

My night ended in disaster, I stayed at Aunty Bella's house and threw up all night, she wasn't best pleased. It took me hours cleaning it up, the smell lingered for days. Not as long as the headache I'd acquired.

I still felt rough on the Monday morning but I had to go to the YTS. Every time I hit a brick with the hammer, I felt my brain shake in my head. St Marie's old school building was falling down and we were informed that we would be moving premises. Our new location was Simms Cross old school. This was ironic, Simms Cross was my old infant school. St Marie's was knocked down some time later and was replaced with a characterless new housing estate. These estates were popping up everywhere. Any spare piece of land was being filled with them. The population of Widnes was growing fast. One such estate was 'Hornet Close Estate.' It was nicknamed Spam city. It was so called because the houses were so pricey, people would put themselves in debt just to say they lived there and would be left with no money for food at the end of every month... except for Spam. Spam was cheap and affordable.

Simms Cross old school was a huge Victorian building. It was in the middle of the Town Centre and was only two minutes walking distance from our old house in Sinclair Avenue, the reason for me attending there.

I was quite sad to leave St Marie's, mainly because we'd done some brickwork in the building and signed our names in the concrete. We thought it would be like a time capsule and would be there for years to come, for other generations to admire. Our work and signatures were lost forever when the building was demolished.

I thought Simms Cross was a listed building, any work we signed here would surely last forever, it couldn't be knocked down... so we thought. On the first day in our new home we were shown to a classroom for an induction. I couldn't believe it, of all the rooms they could have picked in this huge building, they picked this one. It was my very first classroom, as I sat there listening to our tutor rambling on, the memories came flooding back. All I could see was Miss Lidgate, my first teacher. She was small, in her sixties with jet-black hair, always tied back and wore national health glasses. A thinking mans Mrs. Harrison, without the dog.

My first day at school was awful, I recall Madge waving to me as she was leaving with tears in her eyes. I didn't know what was happening, I thought I was been given away for being naughty;

'Don't leave me mum... I'll be good, mum...' I screamed.

Madge started to walk back in my direction but was ushered away by Mr. Hignett who'd seen this a thousand times before. I watched her disappear into the distance, I felt alone. Miss Lidgate picked me up by the arm and sat me at my desk;

'Stop crying you silly boy.' She had the sympathetic values of a hammer, she was a tough old bird.

I eventually calmed down and can still recall the relief I felt when Madge came back for me at three-thirty that day. My time in Miss Lidgate's class never got any better. I was left-handed, I'd inherited this from Madge. Back then, being left-handed was also called 'Gammy-handed' and teachers wanted to encourage you to use your right hand instead. I say encourage, Miss Lidgate had her own way of making sure I never used my left hand when writing.

'Stop writing everybody.' She shouted at the top of her voice. We all froze.

'Now all hold your pencils in the air.' She continued. She then walked slowly around the classroom, looking at our pencils. It became apparent she was looking which hand we were holding them in. She came to me and stopped;

'Put your hand down.' She snapped at me. She looked around the room and shouted in the direction of Adam Sant;

'You boy, go to the cloak room and get me a scarf.' Adam jumped up and scurried towards the door.

'Walk boy and pick your feet up.' She snarled at him.

He came back with a pink wooly scarf, he handed it to Miss Lidgate and went back to his seat. She then ordered me to the front of the class. She told me to put my left arm by my side and tied the scarf around my torso and arm, I couldn't move my left arm, it was clamped. I had no choice but to write with my right hand. It took me a while but I got used to it eventually. Because of this I am now Ampi... Ambedex... Ampedex... Able to write with both hands. Even now, if I ever pick up a pen with my left hand, I have a little peak over my shoulder and expect Miss Lidgate to be stood there with a pink scarf in her hand, shaking her head in dissaprovement.

The best memories I have of Simms Cross were playtime, there were no computers or gadgets to entertain us. We had to make our own fun.

One of my favourites was Rugby without a ball. There would be about fifty kids split into two teams, one team would give one of their players a small bean bag and the other team would have to guess who had it and get it off them before they could touch the wall with the bean bag. You could usually tell who had the bag, he would be the one holding his mid-rift heading directly for the wall, while the other twenty-four kids would be trying to protect him. For anyone watching it must have looked like we'd all gone mad, fifty kids aimlessly running around tackling each other and not a ball in sight.

Red Rover was a popular game, even the girls joined in. Again we would split up into two teams and form a line across the playground holding hands. The other team would be facing us. One team would call someone to try and break the chain of hands, if they broke the chain we could take one of their team, if they didn't they had to join the other team. The winner would be the one with the most players in their team by the end of playtime.

'Best man dead' was without doubt my all time favourite game. The object was simple. When it was your turn, you had to pick a way of dying, hand grenade, rifle, single shot. When you'd picked one, your mate would pretend to kill you with that weapon and you would have to simulate being killed that way. You would be marked out of ten for your acting abilities. I always picked the Tommy gun. I would shake about, pretending to be shot, just like in the war films on television. I always got at least an eight out of ten... I was good, Hollywood was missing out on me.

In my second year at Simms Cross infant school we were told we were moving to a more modern building across the road. It had been a Girls secondary school but was now vacant and ideal. Even though our school was Victorian it was in good shape but too big for the amount of pupils we had. The new school even had a big playing field, it was much better than the old school and much more modern. This was also the time for a lot of the older teachers, including Miss Lidgate to be put out to pasture. We were now in our first year of junior school. A whole wave of new teachers were arriving. Miss Harper was our new teacher, she was about thirty and all the boys fancied her.

We also had a new games teacher Mr.Yeats, he unlike Mr. Hollitt recognised my love of football and made me the captain of the newly formed football team. Every year there would be a five-a-side tournament on the hallowed lawns of Wade Deacon Secondary School. We entered along with every other school in Widnes. We got to the semi-finals and were to face our local rivals, St Bede's catholic school. There was little in terms of distance between the two schools. Simms Cross was a Protestant school, or 'Proddy Dog,' as the 'Catlicks' used to call us. We were getting beat with five minutes to go, my Wembley moment arrived, I took on two of their players and put the ball in the bottom left hand corner, Mr.Years went mad with joy. We got beat on penalties and never made the final but this was our first year of entering. We felt proud of our achievements and Mr.Yeats had medals made with our names on, he paid for them with his own money. I'd started to love school but because of things happening at home, my timekeeping was poor.

'Andy... Andy, are you still with us mate?' Asked my YTS tutor;
'You look miles away.' He continued.
'Sorry, I was just thinking.' I answered, still trying to get Miss Lidgate out of my head.

The bricklaying was coming on fine, Rigger and I had built a few brick fire- places for people and garden walls, we even put foundations in first... who would have thought it. I was approaching my last two months of the scheme and would have to start looking for work. My tutor put me in touch with Halton Borough Council regarding an apprenticeship. I had the interview, it went well. They offered me a five- year course, at the end I would be a qualified bricklayer. It was only Forty pounds a week but would give me a good career. This is where again, my aptitude for making bad decisions raised its ugly head.

Madge informed me they were taking people on at the Golden Wonder crisp factory, where she herself had worked. It paid the Princely sum of Ninety-two pounds a week. I jumped at the chance and turned down the apprenticeship, if only I knew then...

It was two weeks before I reached my Eighteenth birthday, I was to start work at 'The Crispy' in the New Year, things were looking good. I didn't know it then, but starting work there would initiate the worst chain of events in my life.

It was Riggers Eighteenth and we all decided to go out on the town for the first time, we were men now and was going to play with the big boys. I wore my Farah slacks and Ben Sherman shirt. I called at Donna's house to borrow some of Peter's expensive aftershave;
'My little brother's going the pub.' She beamed.

Rigger, three other mates and I were walking down Widnes high street with a swagger, looking at our reflections in the shop windows, for confirmation on how good we looked. We approached the Gamebird, anyone who was anyone went there, we'd heard the stories and couldn't wait to finally get in. We got to the bar, stood with our chests out and in our best manly voices demanded;

'Five pints of Lager please.'

'Got any ID.' The smug barmaid asked us.

Our bubble had been well and truly burst. We assured her we were old enough but she wouldn't serve us, Rigger started to make a bit of a fuss about it. Before we knew it, we were picked up by the scruff of our necks and threw out on the pavement by three Bouncers.

'And don't fucking come back.' The bouncer snarled. He was about six foot four, bald and built like a brick shit house.

We all walked up Dundalk Road heading back towards Ditton, we were embarrassed about being knocked back, we felt stupid. We asked Madge to get us some cans of lager from the Off-licence and celebrated Riggers birthday in my bedroom. We told everyone we'd had a great night in the Gamebird and even went on to the Landmark nightclub, they were suitably impressed, if only they'd have known.

My own Eighteenth birthday was one day away, Donna called to the house with my presents. Hers were always the presents I looked forward too the most. She always put thought into them, this time was no exception. She bought me a pair of 501 jeans. I'd wanted a pair for ages but couldn't afford them. Madge bought me a tankard with 'Eighteen' on, and to my surprise there was fifty pounds in the tankard. I asked her where she got the money from;

'I've been saving for your birthday, it'll have to be for Christmas as well though.' She told me.

I didn't mind, I still had presents from my dad. It was traditional in the Karalius family for your dad to buy you your first legal pint. I went down to grans' house but dad wasn't in. Gran told me he wouldn't be long, I sat there with gran and uncle Brian, they never mentioned my birthday, perhaps they were pretending not to know until dad came back and they'd all shout... Surprise and lavish me with all my presents. Dad came in about twenty minutes later;

'Happy birthday son.' He said matter-of-factly, he then threw an envelope in my direction, he continued;

'Hundred and fifty quid... that's for Christmas as well, I didn't get a card. I don't bloody believe in 'em... they're a bloody rip off.'

Madge

'Thanks, do you fancy a pint and a game of pool at the Queens?' I asked. The Queens was a pub in the next street to grans' house.

'Sorry mate, I've got to go back out. I've got some business to take care of.' So much for tradition then.

I was about to get up to go when Brian called me back and handed me a Twenty- pound note;

'Happy birthday, this is from me and yer gran, we didn't buy a card th....'

'I know, they're a bloody rip off.' I interrupted. I thanked them and left. I got the customary grunt from gran from behind her newspaper.

I couldn't help but notice some weeks later Vin's son was celebrating his fourteenth birthday and everyone including dad had bought him a card.

'Horses for courses.' I suppose. As dad used to say.

I went to the Queens and bought my own first legal pint. It was only a couple of weeks ago I'd been asked for ID at the Gamebird, I couldn't have looked any older but I was served straight away. It must be a sixth sense only barmaids possess, they must know if you're under age or not. Or perhaps it was the way I acted, I was natural. I sat and drank my pint, I had over two hundred pounds in my pocket but there were two things I wanted more than anything, my dad and a card.

For the first time ever I had money to buy Christmas presents. That's the other bad thing about your birthday being so close to Christmas, not only do you get one big present to cover both events but you end up spending most of the money you received for your birthday on Christmas presents for everyone else.

I bought Madge an Oil Of Ulay gift set and a box of After Eight mints, she loved them and would sit eating them whilst watching Coronation Street. I used to joke with her that she shouldn't be eating them at that time, Coronation Street was on at Seven-Thirty and she clearly should wait until after Eight O'clock to eat them. It was the law, or it should be. How can you eat After Eight mints at half past seven? I decided to give her something I never could before, money. I gave her Fifty pounds in a card, she started to cry and said;

'I can't take this, this means I've got you nothing, you've just give me the fifty pounds back I gave you for your birthday.'

I gave her a hug and said;

'Don't worry mum... the card and Tankard was all I wanted.'

She wiped her face and smiled, she opened her After Eights and we sat and ate every one of them until we felt sick.

That Christmas in Parbold Court was one of the best I can remember, nothing of any note happened, it was just normal and our house, no matter where it was we rarely did normal.

The new-year came and I was about to start work in two weeks time. I had one week of my YTS to complete. We didn't do much, we couldn't learn any more in one week that we haven't covered in the previous year, we just used to sign in and go to the Market pub for a game of pool. This was the second time in my life I would be saying goodbye to Simms Cross old school.

I did briefly go back some years later and nearly got arrested for my troubles. It became headline news locally that the school was to be demolished. It became apparent that a new super-market was to be built on the site, it was claimed the school was becoming a danger to the public because of its age and would be knocked down. I was building a garden wall at my house and decided it would be appropriate to take a brick from my first classroom and incorporate it in my wall.

As I was climbing over the safety fences to enter the half demolished school, a police car stopped and two policemen got out of the car;

'What are you doing sir? You do know you're trespassing?'

I explained what I was doing and to my surprise they let me carry on, I took one brick. I thanked the police officers and went on my way. My wife said I was mad. I laid the brick in the middle of the wall… Every time I look out of my living room window I can see my own little piece of Simms Cross old school.

The Supermarket was built, they erected a statue of two children to indicate what once stood there but that was an empty gesture according to most of the general public. The project was doomed from the start. The store had only been open for a week when a young boy was killed by the traffic caused by the new store. The Supermarket was at fault according to many people, in truth it wasn't their fault but people needed someone to blame for this terrible accident. People boycotted the store and there was a huge floral tribute for the young boy. As time went by more and more people started to go back to the store and the floral tributes became less and less each year. I have children myself and couldn't imagine the pain that poor mother must have endured.

Like everything else in my life that comes to an end, I felt sad to be leaving YTS course but all good things as they say. It was the eve of my first six-two shift at the Crispy. I went to bed at ten-thirty but couldn't sleep with excitement and worry. I was embarking on another chapter of my life.

CHAPTER TEN

FACTORY LIFE.

I never realised it before I started writing this book, but I always associate my memories with colour. Good memories I subconsciously see the colour pink surrounding the memory. Average memories, the colour blue and bad memories are accompanied by black and grey. The best way I can put this is when I was describing Miss Lidgate in the previous chapter, I saw grey and black but immediately went to purple and pink when I was relating to Mr.Yeats and the football tournament.

I don't know if this is unique to myself or it's how everyone associates their memories. What I do know is this next part of my life would become like a mis-coloured rainbow, again going from black to pink and pink to black in an instant, with some blue in between.

I got up at five am, I was ready for my first real days work. The Crispy was a short walk from our house and would take no longer than ten minutes. It was a freezing, dark morning, the ground was icy. I must have been mad, I never knew there were two five O'clocks in one day, at least I'd be home at two and get some sleep.

I arrived at the factory with fifteen minutes to spare. The night shift was just finishing, there must have been one hundred people on each shift. We would alternate shifts, one week six-two. The next week two-ten, which would become my favorite shift. Golden Wonder was one of the biggest employers in the town, everyone knew some one who worked there at some time or other.

The supervisor shouted me into her office. She was about thirty or so with short brown hair and the body of a teenage boy. I could tell by the

Madge

way she spoke to me that she didn't like me. It turns out she didn't like men at all, if you know what I mean? I was given a contract for twenty-six weeks, this was so they didn't have to give you holidays. If they employed you any longer, by law they had to class you as a permanent employee. We were only Temps, I didn't mind being a temp. Every six months or so, we would be finished with a wad of money, even though they didn't give us any physical holidays, they had to pay us for them. So when we finished we would have our week in hand, the week we'd just worked and holiday pay, it was great. Then after four weeks they would call you back to work and start all over again.

The permanent staff looked down on the temps. The 'perms' were mainly women in their fifties and sixties, they got the nickname 'The Blue Rinse Mafia.' due to the way they'd keep reminding us that we were only temps and they could have us finished if we didn't pull our weight. It was like a world ruled by women.

I was walked down a long corridor, with each step the mechanical noise was getting louder and louder until the supervisor opened the double doors that led into the production plant. It was like something from Charlie and the Chocolate Factory. Every one wore white peaked caps and long white coats.

As we walked through the plant to where I would be working, people where looking me up and down, the younger girls were whispering and giggling to each other as I passed, I wasn't sure if they were laughing at me, or because they thought I wasn't bad looking. We arrived at a table with three compartments in, one compartment would hold ready salted bags of crisps, the other two cheese and onion and salt and vinegar.

'This is Ronnie, he'll show you what to do, what is your name?' She asked.

'Andy Ka....'

'I don't need your second name mate... Andy will do.' She snapped.

'Take no notice of her mate, she like that with everyone.' Ronnie assured me.

Ronnie was to become a good friend. He was a big guy and worked as a bouncer at the 'Landmark' nightclub. He acquired the nickname 'Uncle Fester' because of his resemblance to the character from the Adams family television series. He was one of eight children and lived in an area colloquially known as 'The Bronx.' There were a lot of decent families, like Ronnie's who lived there but there were an element of hardcore people who gave the area a bad name. It was said they could take the wheels off a car quicker than any professional pit stop team. It was an estate you wouldn't venture into alone after dark. To be fair, that was some years ago and the area has lost its bad reputation. Like the rest of the town, it's progressed.

Ronnie's house became the meeting place before we went out. We would all meet there on a Thursday night and wait for Ronnie to get washed and changed. I would sit in the front room with his mum and dad and watch The Crystal Maze, a games show in the mid-nineties. It would drive Ronnie's dad mad. The object of the game was to complete certain tasks against the clock, if they did they would receive a crystal;

'Where do they get these people from?' He would say.

'They're bloody idiots.'

Ronnie's house was always full, his sisters would be also getting ready in the back room with their mates. Little did I know then but my future wife was one of the girls getting ready in the next room. Our paths have always crossed ever since we were kids, but we never noticed each other. We went to the same weddings, her mum and dad lived just four doors away from Donna's house in Saxon Terrace. The strangest encounter is when we were kids. At the bottom of gran Karalius' back garden was an entrance into a secret world. It was a passageway that led nowhere, it was sandwiched between the back garden's of Egypt Street and Rose Street which ran parallel. I thought only I knew of this secret passageway, it was littered with old bicycle frames and rubbish bags but to me it was a whole different world. It was here where I saw a young girl with scruffy blonde hair, a bit older than me. How did she know of this world? It turns out that little girl was my future wife, her aunties house backed on to the passageway and she would play there when visiting.

Maybe we were always meant to meet? In the stars so to speak. I don't know about that but I do know that our lives interweaved over the years without us even knowing.

Three doors up from Ronnie's house lived his granddad. He was about Eighty years of age and Ronnie had a wonderful relationship with him. I was envious of that. Both mine were dead before I was born, a granddad should be an influential part of any child's life. They say you can't miss what you've never had. Perhaps that's true? But it doesn't stop you wanting what you've never had. I missed not having a granddad.

I read Ronnie's granddad's obituary in the local paper a couple of years ago. I'd not seen Ronnie for some time but felt really sorry for his loss. He loved his granddad.

Obituaries are an odd thing. I say odd because it's only when you reach a certain age that you feel the need to read them… just to see if you know anyone who's died. Uncle Brian and gran Karalius only ever bought the Widnes Weekly News to read the obituaries. Gran, so she could see yet another old friend had passed on. She would then tell us stories related to the deceased. Another way to tell her now legendary tales. Brian had a different motive altogether, he was a professional mourner. He would look for people who'd died and if he remotely knew them or even passed them in the street at some point, that would qualify him to attend the funeral. He loved a good funeral and said they were some of the best do's he'd ever been to.

'You should have been a bloody undertaker.' Dad would say to him.

The shifts were playing havoc with my body clock. I'd just get used to the two-ten shift and the week was over and we were thrown onto six-two. One particular early shift I was knackered, I'd been out with Ronnie the night before and got home late. I arrived home after my shift at two O'clock and went straight to bed, I asked Madge to wake me up at teatime. I recall her shouting me but went back to sleep. I woke up some time later, it was dark. I turned over and looked at my alarm clock, it was a digital clock and displayed the time in big red numbers. It read 6:12;

'Shit.' I shouted, I was late for work. I was convinced it was morning, I ran down stairs and into the living room. Madge was watching the telly, that was odd, she was usually in bed at that time in the morning. She looked at me but said nothing, I ran out the house, putting my coat on scurrying down the path. I then noticed kids playing football under the streetlight. This was all wrong, I normally don't see a living soul this time of a morning… maybe the odd milk float but it was never this busy. It was starting to register, I stopped a passer bye and asked them the time. I then asked them was morning or night.

He looked at me oddly, he must have thought I was mad.

'Night time mate.'

I felt stupid, I was sure it was morning. At least I wasn't late for work, in fact I was early… about eleven and a half hours early. I asked Madge why she didn't tell me. She was in hysterics and found it quite funny. I hated that shift.

Two-ten was my favorite shift. We would finish work at ten O'clock, Madge would have my clothes ironed and I would be in the pub for half ten. We would go to the Landmark every night, except for Wednesdays. That was the only day the nightclub didn't open, it's just as well as Wednesday is also known as 'Bally Anne' day. The day when nobody has any money because the week is nearly over. I'm not sure why it's called Bally Anne day.

Monday night at the Landmark was 'Motown' night, Tuesday was 'Country' night and Thursday was known as 'Grab a granny night.' It was so-called because this was the night when the over thirties or 'oldies' would venture out, bless them.

I was doing quite well with the ladies, the permed mullet had long gone and had been replaced with a long spiky gelled look and long side-burns. I copied the hairstyle from Marty Pellow, the lead singer of the prominent pop group Wet Wet Wet. The girls used to say I looked like him, as a result, barely a night went by when I didn't end up accompanying a different girl home. One night, I met my match, my nemesis. For my own safety I will refer to her as Jane, any similarity to the name 'Jeannette' is purely coincidental. A guy came up to me at the bar and asked would I dance with a friend of his. This guy quite obviously 'sat on the other bus,' so I wrongly assumed he was talking about a man. This was a first… even for me.

To my relief I looked in the direction he was pointing, it was a girl. She was alright but not to the standard I was accustomed to, to be honest, the girls were really thin on the ground that night and 'Jane' was getting better looking with every double Vodka and Coke I was consuming. We did a slow dance to Spandau Ballets classic, *'True'*. I asked could I walk her home and she informed me she was driving. She'd drive me home. This was even better, I'd save a Fiver on Taxi fare. We could now get a Doner kebab on the way home. I was a born romantic.

We parked up outside Parbold Court and had a kiss and cuddle. The nights intake of double Vodka's had taken it's toll. I couldn't go any further, so I took her phone number and said I'd ring her the following night.

As with all the phone numbers I'd collected over the months, it found it's way into the kitchen bin. I never gave it another thought, until the following Friday. I was stood in my usual spot with Ronnie and Ryan, Ryan and I had become inseparable. He also worked at the Crispy and lived in Ditton. He was a good-looking lad, we were a big hit in the Landmark. We stood in the corner, occasionally checking our reflection in the tinted mirrors, Ryan was dating a girl from Ireland, so was more careful with his exploits than I.

Out of nowhere, Jane stormed up to me and started screaming;

'You said you were gonna' phone me… I waited all night, you bastard.'

With that, she threw a drink all over my brand new next shirt. I was gutted, I'd just paid thirty-five pounds for it. For weeks after, every pub I went in she was there. At first it was flattering, my very own stalker! It wasn't long before things would become more sinister… frightening.

I'd just finished another two-ten shift and arrived home at about 10:15. I walked in the living room, Madge had a weird look on her face, I then heard the sound of a teacup being stirred in the back kitchen. I looked at Madge again, this time more inquisitively, before I could say anything, to my horror, in walked Jane holding three cups of tea;

'Hiya love, good shift?' She said with a sickly smile. Madge then went on;

'You didn't tell me you had a girlfriend Andrew.'

I couldn't believe my fucking ears, I was already pissed off because the Landmark wasn't open. This rounded it off perfectly. They both were sat looking at me with stupid smiles on their faces. I didn't know what to do, I couldn't say anything in front of Madge. Jane was obviously a nut case and probably had a gun, or a knife at the very least. I suggested we went for a drive in her car, I'd let her down gently. Try to appeal to her better nature, if she had one.

We got into her blue mini and I told her to drive towards the town centre, I may have needed witnesses. Instead of turning right towards the town, she turned left. I was contemplating jumping out the car.

'Where are we going Jane?' I asked with a nervous quiver in my voice.

She never answered, she leaned forward and turned the volume up on the radio. She started to sing along with the song that was playing, it was *'You'll never stop me from loving you'* by *Sonia*, a pop singer in the late eighties. She was shaking her head to the music and laughing like a mad woman. I looked out of the passenger window in sheer panic. We eventually arrived at 'Pecks Hill,' a renowned hot spot for couples parking up and doing their 'business.' The car park was empty, Pecks Hill is as remote as you could get in Widnes, we were miles from anywhere. She parked the car and turned the engine off and started unbuttoning her blouse. I told her to stop and that we needed to talk.

The headlights of another car turned into the car park. It was the police. They parked next to Jane's car. One of the officers got out, Jane quickly buttoned up her blouse and lowered the window. They told us to move on, I was relieved. Jane was quiet and dropped me back home, she never said a word as I got out of the car, she just screeched off into the distance. She was seriously disturbed.

The final straw with Jane was one Thursday night coming out of the club. I had a girl on my arm and was walking towards the Pizza parlor, we started to cross the road, it was raining and we had a coat over our heads, I couldn't get my hair wet, the Marty Pellow look would have been ruined. From nowhere a car was hurtling towards us, we jumped out of the way. It was a blue mini… She'd tried to run me over. Other people saw what happened. The next day I went to the police and told them what had been happening. They didn't have a lot of sympathy but told me they would talk to Jane.

I never saw her for months, until one night in Players nightclub. She was with some lad, when she seen me she started kissing this lad and then looked at me, I think she must have thought I would be jealous. I was relieved but I couldn't help but feel sorry for the poor bastard she was with.

This was around the time when I noticed deterioration in Madge's health. She couldn't walk to far without having to stop and catch her breath. She went to the doctors, it became apparent she had Angina. The doctor told Madge she must stop smoking.

It also became apparent where Madge had got my birthday money from. We were sat in the living room on a Friday afternoon, Madge seemed uneasy. I asked her what was wrong? She said nothing was the matter. All of a sudden there was a loud knock on the front door;

'Don't answer it.' Madge whispered.

The door knocked again, this time even louder. I'd had enough, I ran to the door and opened it. There were two men stood there, the first man was about six foot with long silver hair and thick expensive glasses. He wore a long camel skin over-coat. The second man was dressed in a leather jacket and was somewhat younger;

'What do you want?' I asked.

'I'm Mr. Livingstone, your mum has not paid me for three weeks. I want my money.'

He was a loan shark. Madge had borrowed £75 pounds from him, fifty of which she gave me for my birthday;

'How much does she owe you?' I asked.

He informed me she owed him £150. The cheeky bastard went to walk in the house, I put my hand on his chest and told him to wait outside. I ran upstairs and got the shoebox from under my bed where I kept my wages. I only had eighty pounds, I ran back down stairs to the front door and told him I would pay him the rest the following week. As he held out his hand to take the money I dropped it on the garden path. He looked up at me through his thick glasses, the younger guy started to walk towards me, Livingstone stopped him and told him to pick up the money.

Despite still owing him seventy pounds, we never saw Mr. Livingstone again after that day. I heard some days later he and his henchman had been mugged on the Ditton estate and he was to scared to come back again. I wasn't sad to hear that and most of the area wanted to throw a party in honour of his demise, he was a leach who preyed on vulnerable people. It was said that four youths robbed him, one of which was a coloured youth… but I couldn't possibly comment on that.

CHAPTER ELEVEN

Jersey Royals.

Every Thursday afternoon was payday, we would go to the hatch in the canteen and receive our hard earned wages. I say hard earned but I'd moved away from packing crisps and worked my way up bag stamping. I would stamp the date on the multi-bags, you had to be quick to keep up with the incessant packers. It had a big advantage, there were four of us but only two on the shop floor at any one time. We would work for half an hour, then have a break for half an hour. We only really worked twenty hours a week. The blue rinse mafia hated it but as long as the job was getting done the bosses didn't seem to mind.

In those days we would get our wages in a pay packet, this brought it's own problems. Men would lose their entire wages playing cards. I played but knew my limits, I'd seen first hand the effects gambling could have. If I lost more than ten pounds, I would get out.

One particular day my luck was well and truly in, the game was three-card brag, a great game if you're lucky but a cruel game if you're not. My cards were dealt, I went 'blind.' That means I was betting on my hand without seeing it, anyone who had seen their cards would have to pay double the stake to stay in the game. It was a great way of building up the pot. After going one pound blind three times, I decided to look at my hand. There were six players in the game, four had thrown their cards in. Dougie French wasn't budging, he looked smug. He didn't stay in the game if he had nothing. I took a sneak at my cards… I couldn't believe what I was seeing, I had a prile, 'three queens.' There was over thirty pounds in the pot. I bet another two pounds, Dougie did like wise, still smiling smugly. I then raised the bet to five pounds, my heart was pounding, I had a great hand but there were three more possible hands that could beat me. Three kings, three aces or three three's, the best hand you could get in Brag. Dougie may have one of them. He raised the bet to ten pounds, I was shitting myself, my mouth was dry. He must have sensed my anxiety;

'To rich for ya' Andy mate?' He said with an air of arrogance.

The pot was now over fifty pounds, over half my wages. I paid another ten pounds and told him to turn his cards over.

'Read 'em and weep.' He said turning over his cards one at a time.

He turned the ace of clubs first. 'SHIT' I thought, it seemed an eternity before he turned his second card. As if in slow motion he turned the card, it was the two of clubs, followed by the three… he had a running flush, a great hand but it doesn't beat a prile. I threw my cards over and jumped in the air. Dougie's face turned white, he'd lost over twenty-five quid. He stood up and simply said;

'Fuck off.' Before storming out of the canteen. I had over thirty pounds in coins, so next game I decided to go blind about ten times, to get rid of some of the slummy.

What happened next was remarkable. The cards were dealt again, Matt Pitchillingy, or Pitchy, as he was better known, had replaced Dougie at the table. Like me, his granddad was Lithuanian. I don't know why he bothered playing, every time he got a good hand he would go bright red and give the game away. I went blind again, this time two people stayed in, Pithcy sat there looking like a big red tomato, he obviously had a good hand and Paul, one of the supervisors sons. There was over fifty pounds in the pot again, ten pounds of it was mine, so I decided to have a look… three two's, I started laughing and told the two remaining players what I had. I liked Pitchy and didn't want to take any more of his wages, he immediately threw his cards in. Paul didn't believe me, the dickhead said I was bluffing. I didn't mind taking his money, so I carried on betting. In twenty minutes I'd won nearly twice my wages.

Men's wives went to the factory to complain about their husband's losing all their wages. The card school was banned, I didn't care, I'd already won.

As well as Pot Noodles, I can't stand Wotsits. Not because I ate too many, I dislike them for a whole different reason. The Widnes factory never made Wotsits, they were made in a different factory down south. They were then sent to our factory to be packed. Several of the lads would put Wotsits up their nose and in their ears, they never went out for consumption but the thought of them sticking out of someone's nose put me off for life.

As well of Ryan's girlfriend and her sister Triona, there was an influx of Irish girls arriving in Widnes and many of them started working at the Golden Wonder. They lived in Bed and Breakfast's in the town centre. Triona attracted some of my attention, I don't know why, she wasn't my type at all and I wasn't hers. I took her out a few times. I think it was so I would be part of the gang. There was Ryan and his girlfriend, Danny, who also worked at the crispy started to go out with one of the other Irish girls and me with Triona. We had some good nights out, particularly on St Patrick's night, but I never saw Triona as long term.

My second stint at the crispy was coming to an end. Danny and myself, along with five other lads decided that we'd go to Jersey in the Channel Islands working as potato pickers until the crispy called us back.

One by one people were dropping out, Danny and I were the only ones left. Unperturbed, we decided to go anyway. Madge wasn't happy, she said she'd never seen me again. That was ridiculous, I was only going for a few weeks. She said we'd make our millions over there and never come back… how wrong she was.

Danny was a funny character, he was the joker in the pack. If it was your birthday in the crispy and he and Ronnie found out, you were in trouble. They found out that it was my nineteenth birthday, they wrapped me up in cellophane and put me in the luggage compartment of the number 28 bus, then Ronnie carried me over his shoulder through the town centre to Donna's house in Saxon Terrace. We knew it was Danny's birthday and told him we were going to tell Ronnie. Danny waited for the right opportunity and blurted out that it was someone's birthday on the table, the canteen went quiet and Ronnie asked who was getting it today? Danny immediately looked over at Pitchy, he went bright red and it wasn't even his birthday. Ronnie tied Pitchy up and put him in a skip, then took his car for three days. Danny back healed that one all right.

I'd never flown in a plane before and was quite nervous at the thought, even though it was only a forty or so minute flight. We were dropped off at Manchester Airport by Danny's brother-in-law. We checked in and went to the departure lounge. Danny was winding me up, he knew I was nervous. The planes looked huge, it made me feel a bit better, until a small plane chugged out of the hanger. Danny joked that it was our plane… it was no joke, it was our plane.

We got on the plane, it was tiny. I said to Danny it reminded me of one of those Island planes you see in the Movies, the pilot was always Irish, unshaven, dirty white shirt and a rolled up cigarette hanging out of his mouth. The joking was settling me down a little bit. Then a voice came over the tannoy;

'Good afternoon, this is Captain O'Malley….'

That was it, I was getting off… Danny pulled me back and told me we'd be fine, the flight was a bit bumpy but not as bad as I thought.

In fact it was Danny who had a bad flight, he got a blinding headache. Poetic justice, I thought, for winding me up all day.

We arrived in St Hellier via Taxi, it's the capital of the Island. Jersey is a lovely, picturesque place. You get the feeling it's not quite sure of it's own identity. It's owned by the United Kingdom but is closer to France, even the weather couldn't make up its mind. Within the first two hours of being on the Island, it rained, snowed until eventually the sun was beating down on the beautiful beach.

The first thing we had to do was find somewhere to stay. We never pre-booked anywhere, Danny had been there before and assured me we would get accommodation quite easily. What he didn't tell me was, his first visit was ten years previous when he was nine years of age. The first Hotel we went to was huge. Danny told me to let him do the talking as he was practically a local. We arrived at the check in desk and Danny asked;

'How much for a double room with two single beds?'

The guy at reception looked us up and down, he had a French accent. He had a face like he was sniffing dog shit;

'Seventy five pounds.' He said nonchalantly.

'Great, can we book in for a week please.' Danny replied, with a smug wink in my direction.

'That will be £525.00… in advance.' The French guy continued.

The colour drained from Danny's face, he thought it was seventy-five pounds for the week, not for one night. He looked back at me, I found it hysterical and in a very low drawl through tightened lips he said to me;

'Grab the fucking bags… and run.'

He then turned back to the French guy, smiled and ran outside. Everyone in the hotel stopped and looked at me, I stood there with four bags in my hands and simply said to the French receptionist who was now looking at me with total disdain;

'You'll have forgive my friend, he's practically a fucking local.' Before calmly walking out the hotel, only to find Danny in stitches about forty yards down the road.

We eventually found a small B&B on St Hellier's sea front. The front of the house was bright pink. We knocked on the door and waited for a while. The door finally opened, there stood an old lady in her seventies. I asked if she had any rooms available. She told me she had two at twenty pounds.

'A night.' I stressed, looking at Danny. He just smiled.

It became clear while this guesthouse had vacancies when no-body else on the Island did. The room was poky, it had two single beds and one wardrobe. It looked and smelt like my gran Karalius' bedroom, clean but very dated. We had little choice. Our time in Jersey wasn't getting off to a great start. At least we could go and find work the following day. Not before we hit the town, sample what the Island had to offer in the way of clubs and more importantly… girls.

Jersey is a tax haven for affluent people and it was apparent everywhere, yachts in the small harbour. Ferrari's and Rolls Royce's everywhere you looked. You had to have money to live here, that was something we had little of. We had enough for a weeks stay if we couldn't find work but that was basic living.

We eventually found a nightclub, it was small but not bad. Nightclubs closed at 1am in Jersey, one hour before we were used to on the 'Mainland'. To my amazement, that's what everyone called England, then why wouldn't they? Jersey was an Island after all… off the mainland. It just sounded odd to me.

As the night went on I could see Danny becoming more drunk by the minute. He was talking to the barmaid most of the evening and informed me he may be back late to the B&B.

'I've pulled mate… she wants me.' He drawled.

I didn't mind one bit. I was a hit in the club and was talking to a few girls. My options were soon to be scuppered. I went over to the bar to tell Danny I was going for a drive with one of the girls but he was lay flat on his back in front of the bar. I had to throw him in a taxi and take him back to the B&B. I was pissed off, here I was sat in an old persons bedroom at 11;45 at night, nowhere to go and Danny snoring his head off in the next bed.

The following day we went to find work, we never did our homework. The Jersey Royals we came here to pick weren't ready for harvesting for another six weeks and we didn't have enough money for another six days. This 'working' holiday was turning into a disaster. We quickly decided to spend just two more days on the Island and head back home with our tails between our legs. So much for Madge's prediction. I rang Madge to tell her I'd be home soon but she had some news for me. Donna was pregnant and

Madge

expecting her first child, Madge was delighted. Despite not liking Peter very much, she always wanted to be a granny. She asked me how I felt, I was pleased for Donna but it wasn't going to change my life that much, I was more concerned with the current predicament I was in.

Danny had brought a camera with him, he wanted me to take pictures of him in exactly the same places he'd had his photo taken ten years previous. We spent most of the day doing so. There was nothing in the way of entertainment that night in the B&B so we bought two notepads and entertained ourselves. For three hours we played writing down as many different names for penis and vagina as we could think of. It was very sad but with hilarious results. For any women reading this… I'm sorry, it's a man thing!

We awoke next morning to what was to be our last day on this ill-fated holiday. Our money was low, if we took it easy we could afford one last night out before jetting off the following morning. Our money was so low that we either ate or drank alcohol. we'd just ate our breakfast at the guesthouse so we decided on the latter. We were surrounded by affluence but didn't have a pot to piss in between us, it was a horrible feeling, seeing Rolls Royce cars passing us by… 'One day mate.' Danny said, still with his ever-present optimism.

We went to the second of only two night clubs on the Island, Danny couldn't go back to the other one where he ended up flat on his back. There was a singing competition, the prize was a gallon of bear. Danny jumped at the chance. While everyone else were singing their hearts out. Danny got up and did his hysterical impersonation of *'Living Doll'* by Cliff Richard. He won hands down. We had four free pints each… they were more than welcome. The holiday from hell finished on a high note. We even got a Doner Kebab on the way back to the B&B, a vegetarian one, we couldn't afford the meat.

True to form, getting home was not going to be easy. There were delays at Manchester airport. The only way we could get home was to fly to Gatwick, then a long coach drive from Euston station in London. We had little choice. We didn't have a penny left. We did consider sleeping on the beach, we heard that the Police would deport anyone doing so, for vagrancy but you would never be allowed back on the Island. That was fine with me, I never intended going back anyway. Danny said his dad would kill if he was sent home for being a tramp, he had a point.

We flew to Gatwick on a real plane, not an Island jalopy. I recall seeing the White Cliffs of Dover for the first time, it was a beautiful sight.

I imagined how fighter pilots must have felt during the second World War, seeing 'home,' knowing they'd be seeing their family soon. We'd not long passed over the Cliffs when we were told to fasten our seat belts. Panic set in, I wrongly assumed that Gatwick was in London and though I was no geography expert, I knew we weren't anywhere near London. I told Danny we were crash landing. Even he panicked a bit, I was looking for a field to land in. Nobody else on the plane had noticed, where they all thick? I looked at the faces of the flight attendants, they were good but they'd been trained not to show any signs of panic in an emergency. We were in trouble, I was about to go and see the captain when we landed safely on the runway at Gatwick Airport. It turns out Gatwick is actually in Hampshire and not London. I told Danny I was just winding him up, I felt a right dickhead.

After a two-hour coach ride to Euston Station and a six-hour wait for another coach to take us to Widnes, we eventually arrived home. I was never so pleased to see Parbold Court. Half way up the path, the door opened and Madge ran down and hugged me. I'd only been away just short of four days… But it did feel a lot longer. To my surprise Al was sat in the living room, I don't know how or when that happened but I was glad to see him again. He asked me how the holiday went, I told them 'almost' the whole story. The next day I saw Al riding up our path on his old black bike. He called me into the kitchen and handed me fifty pounds;

'What's that for?' I asked.

'At least you tried… this is to tide you over until you get back to work.'

That typified the sort of man he was, a true gentleman. I later called at gran Karalius', they weren't even aware I'd been anywhere, that was also typical.

In the summer of that year my niece was born, Stacey. I know everyone says it about their own and I normally think babies are ugly, a cross between Winston Churchill and a chimpanzee. But Stacey was a beautiful baby, a mop of jet-black hair and the smoothest skin I'd ever seen. For the first time ever, a miracle happened that day at Whiston Hospital. Madge, dad, Donna and Peter all in the same room and not a bad word spoken between them. We almost looked like a normal family.

Madge adored her granddaughter and would baby-sit her most days while Donna and Peter worked. I think it gave her something else in her life. Her drinking wasn't like before. She couldn't do it anymore, her health was deteriorating. None of us knew to what degree. She would still drink at Maggie's house at the weekends but a lot less than she used to.

The summers in Parbold Court where great, a real sense of community. Kids playing on the grass, the adults chatting and laughing away over the garden fences. This particular summer was marred by the freakiest accident I've ever seen. One of Maggie's sons, Daley was pretend boxing with another kid. From nowhere next doors dog came running at speed. The dog hit Daley and sent him about six foot in the air, the noise was horrendous, akin to the snapping of a piece of wood. Everyone stopped what they were doing, when Daley eventually landed, his leg was like a huge banana. People couldn't look, it was a horrible break. I felt sorry for Daley, he was only twelve years old and was a lovely lad. He spent almost six months in hospital and never walked the same after. There were calls for the dog to be put down, I understood that, but to be fair it was an accident. The dog was found dead some weeks later, it had been poisoned. That was the sort of neighbourhood we lived in, rightly or wrongly, they believed in an eye for an eye.

The letter came through the door again, Golden Wonder wanted me back. I didn't know it then but this would be my third and final stint at 'The Crispy.'

The usual greetings on our first day back were acknowledged. Most talk was about Danny and I and the 'nightmare in Jersey.' They all found it quite funny, despite everything, I'm glad I went. It was an experience and like Al wisely said… At least we tried.

I was starting to see more and more of Triona. She asked would I like to go to Ireland with her on a holiday. It couldn't be any worse than my last holiday, so I agreed. I was becoming an international jet setter. The Channel Islands, London, now Ireland, the world was my oyster.

Things were going good, then Madge dropped a bombshell. She was moving house again. I didn't want to move away from Ditton but she wanted to go back near the town, to be closer to Donna and Stacey. She had agreed to give our two bed-roomed house up and take up residence in a one bed-roomed upstairs flat in Lowerhouse Lane, the opposite end of the rugby ground to Sinclair Avenue. The fact it only had one bedroom meant I'd have to sleep on the couch, but like it was pointed out to me, I would be twenty years of age next birthday and wouldn't be living with Madge forever. That was fucking news to me, I intended on staying until I was at least forty.

The papers were signed and the move was imminent. The day we left

Parbold Court was bitter sweet, Madge wanted to move to the town but had made many good friends in Ditton, she knew she wouldn't be seeing much of them again.

As we turned away from Parbold Court for the last time, it reminded me of when Madge left Sinclair, she looked out of the back of the taxi and waved to the neighbours, Madge had a tear in her eye. One by one the neighbours went back into the house. In the distance, becoming smaller and smaller was one solitary figure stood waving to Madge, like an orphan seeing her parents driving away for the last time… it was Maggie.

CHAPTER TWELVE

WHEN IRISH EYES ARE...

Moving back near to the rugby ground had its advantages. The Cricketers Arms, otherwise known as 'Leggies' by the locals was directly across from Madge's new flat. This would become my local. It was called Leggies because a previous owner had a wooden leg and he got the nickname, Leggie. The name stuck, unlike his leg.

This was also the time I would have my fifteen minutes of fame, well more like fifteen seconds and it wasn't really fame. I was on the television though. I've already mentioned that despite my sirname, I wasn't a big rugby league fan. I was selective, I would go to the big games and even use my name to my advantage on occasions. I would show some identification at the turnstiles, tell them Vin was my uncle and get to watch the game for free. Strictly speaking I did have an uncle Vin, just not the famous rugby player.

Widnes were playing Wigan on the final day of the season, who ever won the game, won the league title. We were all stood in the Cow Shed, singing our hearts out. It was a close game but Widnes came out on top. The final hooters sounded and all the Widnes fans raced onto the field, I got on Ryan's shoulders, I was cheering like a hypocrite. Later that evening the highlights were shown on television and there I was in full technicolour on Ryan's shoulders in front of the watching millions of viewers.

Ever since I was young I would pick and choose the games I would attend. When we lived in Sinclair Avenue in the 70's. Widnes rugby league club were known as 'The cup kings.' They got to the challenge cup final on four occasions. Mrs Daresbury, who lived across from aunty Fiona and next to aunt Kit would organise coach trips to Wembley. She was chairwoman of the Widnes fan club otherwise known as the 'Chemics.' The name was derived from Widnes being a chemical town. Her son was also the official Widnes mascot. On Wembley day Sinclair Avenue would be full of coaches, everyone adorned in black and white, the colours of their beloved Widnes rugby league club. Madge surprised me when we got to the 1977-cup final against Leeds, she told me we were going to Wembley. I was over the moon, it wasn't Manchester United but it was Wembley.

When we got to Wembley the atmosphere was amazing, a sea of black and white and blue and yellow (Leeds colours.) I never knew so many people lived in Widnes, there can't have been anyone left in the town. Except for Donna, who said she'd rather go out without make-up than watch rugby.

Madge and I were stood right behind a steel pillar, I could hardly see anything. It didn't go un-noticed. A Leeds fan told Madge to lift me over the small fence and watch it with them, she did and I saw the game in full view. The match was evenly paused, until Stuart Wright, a brilliant winger made an uncharacteristic mistake, allowing Leeds to get the decisive try. I cried that day, the occasion got the better of me.

The trip home was great, despite defeat everyone was singing. On every occasion Widnes got to Wembley, they would have a home coming ceremony at the Municipal buildings, or the Town Hall, as it was better known. 1977 was no exception, all the Widnes fans started to shout Stuart Wright's name, he was a great player and that one indiscretion would not ruin their affections for him… even if he did look like a Seventies porn star.

If my scam at the turnstiles didn't pay off, I would climb over the perimeter wall to avoid paying. Once over, you would drop into the urinals. The look on the peoples faces while taking a piss was a picture. On one occasion I'd actually paid to watch Widnes play against Workington Town. It was pouring with rain and the worst game I've ever seen, I decided to climb out, all the gates were locked. As I was half way over the wall a police car stopped and the officer asked what I was doing?

'Climbing out, it's a bad game.' I replied.

The officer shook his head and laughed;

'I've heard everything now.' He said, before driving away.

I didn't mind having to sleep on the settee at Madge's new flat, it wasn't ideal as Madge was a night owl and didn't go to bed until late. When I was on the six-two shifts I would stay at the bed sit with Triona. The owners of the bed sit didn't allow people to stay over. If by chance I was there when the owners wife came to Hoover the rooms, I would have to hide in the tiny wardrobe. This was rarely a problem, until the day I accidentally fell out of the wardrobe and landed flat on my back on the bedroom floor. Triona's face drained with colour. They liked Triona and let her off with a warning.

Christmas 1989 was approaching and we were ready to sail to Ireland. We were going for a week and would arrive back on New Years Day, just in time for aunty Mavis' legendary party.

We arrived at Holyhead sea port on the Island of Anglesey. Like the plane, I had never sailed before, especially across the tempestuous Irish Sea. I drank a little too much and was somewhat worse for wear. I was lucky they let me on the boat at all. Triona persuaded them and that she would look after me, they agreed.

I don't recall much of that first crossing to Dublin, I slept through most of it. I was advised by many people that as an English protestant visiting a very catholic Ireland, there were two things I should not get into conversation about, politics and religion. The troubles in Ireland were still prominent. It was evident, as we walked through the city of Dublin, we passed two burnt out cars. People were just walking past them like it was normal, perhaps it was. Dublin is like most major cities I've visited with one exception, it has a river running through the middle of the high street. The river Liffey, the first thing I noticed was the colour of the water, it was grey with a thick scum floating on the surface. Widnes is on the banks of the river Mersey, so I'm in no position to cast aspersions, it has it's own pollution problems but I'd never seen anything quite like the Liffey.

Triona's parents lived sixty miles inland from Dublin, a small village named Clonaslee, in County Laoise. The bus journey took about an hour and a half. We finally arrived in the village, it was small. It had one shop, a chip shop, a butchers and four pubs, three of which were called Kelly's. To avoid any confusion they named the bars by the owner's first names. Paddy's, Mick's and Eric's, I wasn't quite sure about Eric, that sounded about as Irish as Haggis. Arriving in the tiny village I thought our long journey was over, not a chance. We still had a 'short' walk to Triona's house. I say short, now I know what they mean by 'An Irish mile.' They go on and on. We left our luggage in Mick Kelly's bar and started to walk the long country lane, which would eventually lead to Triona's house.

The house was in fact a small bungalow and was set back off the road in the middle of nowhere. It had a huge back garden where her dad would grow potatoes and chop wood to gain extra income. John, her dad was a typical Irish man, if you put him in a line out with ten other men and was asked to pick the Irish man, you would pick him every time. He was small and thin with a mop of brown hair, his ears stuck out and he had about two teeth in his head. Her mum Bridy was the total opposite. She was small and plump and was very well spoken. I could never understand a word John said, he had a very broad accent.

I was told I would have to sleep in the spare room, they were strong Catholics and didn't believe in co-habituating before marriage. I respected that.

Saturday soon arrived and Triona was excited, there was a big party to be held at Paddy Kelly's bar. We all got ready and started the half hour walk to the village, it was cold and had started to rain, I asked why we just couldn't phone for a taxi. They all laughed at me, I felt like an idiot;

'What?' I said.

'One, we don't own a phone and two, by the time a taxi got here it would be time to come home... there's no taxi's for miles around.' Bridy told me.

I could tell they didn't really like our 'City folk' ways, they thought we had it easy and were spoilt. When we got to the end of the lane I noticed about ten people stood waiting, I was about to ask was this a bus stop but after the taxi comment, I thought better of it. It was sort of a bus stop, more of a car stop. These people would wait for a car to come past and hitch a lift. It didn't matter if you knew them or not, it was the norm. our turn came, I felt a little embarrassed, this was not the done thing in England. In fact you are taught never to take a lift from someone you didn't know. This was a different way of life all together. Time didn't seem to be an issue, everything was done at a methodical pace.

A car pulled up and Triona, her mum and dad and myself got in. it was a tight squeeze, there was eight people squashed in a Ford Escort. We were dropped in the village, literally. I could here the music coming from Paddy's bar. I noticed one man staggering out of the bar, he must have been drinking in there all day, he was plastered. Two police men or 'Garda' as they're known in Ireland had hold of the man, I thought they were taking him to the small barracks at the end of the village to sleep it off. To my amazement, they helped him into his tractor;

'Now careful you go Joe.' One of them shouted to him, before disappearing back into the bar.

Madge

The tractors engine started, I went to cross the road heading towards the bar, Triona's dad grabbed my arm and said;

'Wait one minute… wouldn't want ye killed on yer first visit.'

I didn't know what he meant. It soon became apparent. The tractor started up and turned a full circle before crashing into the ditch across from the bar. I started to run over to help him but again Triona's dad stopped me;

'Don't worry yerself, he'll be fine. Sure he does it every week.'

I couldn't believe my eyes, the man could be dead. We entered the bar and everyone stopped and looked at me. I was big news in the village and everyone wanted to see what the Englishman from the big city looked like. I felt like a film star. People were shaking my hand and buying me drinks. I was half expecting them to ask for my autograph. They were very hospitable and made me feel right at home. The night was going great but once you've heard one Irish song, you've heard the lot but we were having 'The Crack' as they say. I went to the bar to buy our tickets for the New Years Eve party, Paddy Kelly wouldn't take my money;

'You're my guest… put yer money away.' He said with a wink.

I thought me being an English protestant would be a problem in Ireland but they welcomed me like one of their own. Sunday morning, everyone attended church. I explained to John that I didn't frequent the church, unless it was a christening or a funeral. He understood and told me to go and wait in the bar for him. I ordered him a Guinness. When you get a Guinness in England, it's poured and given to you straight away. Not in Ireland, the home of the 'Black Gold,' they pour it and let it stand for about ten minutes to let it settle. In the mean time people would usually have a Whiskey and it was always 'medicinal' of course.

Church was over and the whole congregation would pour into the bar in their best bib and braces. They would much rather be in the bar than the church, they did nothing but slag off the Priest for keeping them in the house of god for longer than he should have. Why go? I always thought religion was like wallpaper, it covered a lot of cracks. I think it was Rudyard Kipling who said;

'If there was no such thing as God, there would be a need to invent one.'

I never mentioned this to John, I kept in mind the sound advice I was given about religion and politics before I left England. Don't get me wrong, I'm not an atheist, I do believe in a higher being. I just don't think it's a big guy in the sky with a white beard and I certainly don't have to go to any church to 'prove' my faith. Not long ago I wasted a full hour of my life watching a documentary regarding 'The Turin Shroud.' Scientist's and philosophers debating the authenticity of the cloth that supposedly blanketed the body of Christ after his death. These were intelligent men and women but not one of them mentioned the possibility of Christ being a clever piece of fiction. I think religion is a good invention, if it helps a person in their darkest hours, that's fine. When it's the cause of wars and people being killed, then that surely contradicts what religion is all about. Enough of my soapbox and the gospel according to Andrew. Here endeth the lesson.

The priest would always come to the bar after mass with a collection box. This wasn't a request, it was a demand. He came to me and shook my hand, everyone stopped and looked at me. Should I be a hypocrite and put money in the box, or stick to my beliefs and decline? The priest thanked me for my ten pounds contribution and the whole congregation nodded in approval. I raised my glass in acknowledgement. I was well and truly accepted, I was practically a catholic. In truth I wanted to run after the priest, jump him from behind and take my ten pounds back.

New Years Eve arrived and the impending party at Paddy Kelly's was the talk of the village. Paddy's bar seemed to have the monopoly on parties, I never even stepped foot in the other bars. How did they stay open? There was one thing to do before the party. I'd been invited to play for the village football team in their annual New Years Eve game against the next village. Clonaslee had not won for the last three years. I think they saw me as their secret weapon. I'd told them I wasn't a bad player and they just took my word for it. Word must have spread, they had the best attendance ever, forty-two spectators lined the pitch that day. The pitch was in a disused farmers field, not the best I've ever played on but it will do. We got changed in a shed, the manager, who also happened to be the local butcher and a member of the I R A political party, threw me a pair of tracksuit bottoms and told me I was on the bench, problem was there was no bench. I stood and watched the first half on the sidelines, it was freezing. We were getting beat two nil, both teams were poor and I couldn't wait to get on, I could wipe the floor with these, they were that bad. The half time team talk was lively, though to be honest I could hardly understand a word the manager was saying. He turned to me and asked where I played? I told him my best position was in midfield;

'Get yerself ready then... yer on.'

There was a buzz in the 'crowd' when they seen me appear for the second half. I once again felt like a celebrity. We kicked off the second half, the ball was immediately passed to me. I looked up to pick my pass, before I could do anything I was clattered to the ground. I was lay on the floor, stood over me was a big Irish man, more suited to rugby than football.

'How's that yer English bastard?' He growled through his beard.

I took the free kick, I purposely sent the ball to the hairy bastard who'd just put me on my arse. He headed towards me with the ball. I took his legs from under him. As he lay on the ground in agony, I went over to him and said;

'How's that you Irish bastard?'

He kept away from me for the rest of the game. I was always taught that football is like life, if someone hits you, hit them back.

There was twenty-five minutes to go and we were still getting beat two nil. I got the ball near the centre circle and took on two players and threaded the ball through to Sean O'Brien, the team captain. He put the ball in the top corner, we were back in the game, our spectators went mad. I was running the midfield and set up Jimmy Flynn for the equaliser. My Wembley moment finally came in a farmer's field in the out back of Ireland. I got the ball and did a one two with Sean, I went to take my shot but was fowled inside the box. We got a penalty in the last two minutes. Sean handed me the ball and told me to take it. I placed the ball on the spot and put it in the bottom corner, sending the goalkeeper the wrong way. It was Roy of the Rovers stuff. The final whistle went soon after. We won 3-2. The big hairy Irish guy came towards me, I thought he was going to punch me. He held out his hand and said;

'Good game English.'

'Good game Irish.' I said back.

I was put on Sean O'Brien's shoulders and paraded all the way back to the pub. That was my best memory of Ireland. I'd been given a new name after that day, 'Gazza.' After Paul Gascoigne, the brilliant English footballer of the day. I didn't drink too much, we had the party to go to on the night.

Madge was very much in my thoughts that night, it was her birthday the following day. I'd never been away for her birthday, I was twenty years of age yet still missed my mum. To be honest the party was like any other night in Paddy's bar. Irish music, followed by… more Irish music. Midnight sounded, everyone wished each other happy new year. I rang Madge and wished her happy birthday. I could hardly hear her through all the noise. She could hear me, it was quiet on that end, she was alone. I felt bad and vowed never to leave her on her own again on her birthday.

To confound my sadness, the next song sang was *'When Irish Eyes Are Smiling.'* What a depressing song. There's a line in it that sings… *'You'll never miss your mothers love, until she's dead and gone.'* How right they were.

I couldn't wait to get home, I love home. It's where I'm comfortable, it's okay getting away every now and then but it's always good to come home. We arrived in Liverpool just after dinnertime. Dad picked us up from the ferry port and dropped me off at home. I gave Madge a hug and gave her the present I'd bought. A bottle of Irish whiskey. Her drinking days were behind her, although she still would indulge every now and then.

My drinking days where very much still ahead of me. Mavis's New Years Day party was looming. Triona said she didn't want to come, she'd drank too much over Christmas and wanted to rest. That was fine by me, maybe I would get lucky with some other girl at the party. Triona was just a means to an end. That sounds harsh, I know. I'd just turned twenty and didn't want to be bogged down, I had a lot of living to do. I got the feeling she wanted to get married and have children at a young age, like her mum and dad. I bet she'd sit in her tiny bedroom in Ireland, planning her life out. I suppose looking back and it's only now as I sit here writing that maybe I was a chip off the old block after all. I was too much like hard work for Triona, she didn't care how her boyfriend looked. She wanted stability and foundation. I was starting to believe my own press. Girls would tell me I was good looking and my head got bigger with every compliment and stability, I was about as stable as a one legged man on a Treadmill.

Despite all of this, Triona and I were to move in together in the coming months. I think we both knew it would never last but I couldn't sleep on Madge's settee forever. It was time I started playing at being an adult. For now at least I was happy and Triona's Irish eyes were smiling.

CHAPTER THIRTEEN

Unlucky For Some.

1990 was a new year. A new decade. The Eighties weren't too bad but I was glad to see the back of them. The Seventies had to be the worst decade in my opinion, a grey decade. The seventies had a lot to live up to, it was in transition. It didn't seem to have any identity, even The Beatles found themselves in disarray. Everything good about the previous decade was turning sour. England won the world cup in 1966. Four years later, the start of the 70's we were humbled. This was the start of things to come for the next ten years. 1990 was also a world cup year, Italy were the hosts. Ryan, his girlfriend Patricia, Triona and myself were going on holiday in Yugoslavia. This is where I thought England had finally reached the Holy Grail of football, the World cup final. More of that later.

I arrived at Mavis's New Years Day party, all the Karalius clan were there. Uncle Derek's family also attended. The party was okay but everyone was winding down after the holidays and were gearing themselves up for work the following Monday. After two cans of lager dad would do his annual rendition of Frank Sinatra. Gran Karalius would complain about the noise and Donna and Peter would turn up fashionably late as usual.

Mavis's next-door neighbour attended this particular year. I noticed him looking closely at people's hands most of the evening, I wondered what the hell he was doing. As well as being an Ambulance man, it turns out he also read people's palms. I'm open minded to most things but I thought this particular way of telling the future was lame. He could see my distain for what he was doing and asked me would I want my palm read? I agreed, what harm could it do. After studying my palm he told me

I would have a rough sea crossing by boat. It was no secret I'd just got back from Ireland and was due to go again, so I dismissed that one. It was also common knowledge that I played a lot of football, so his next revelation was no surprise. He foretold that I would have an accident while playing football, to my right leg. I laughed it off, as I got up and went to walk to the kitchen to get myself another drink, he shouted me back;

'Remember what I've said… be careful.'

I laughed again, this time I felt a little scared, he looked concerned. As the night went on I soon forgot about the telling of my future.

Like everyone else, I was due to go back to work at the Crispy. I didn't know it then but my time as a Golden Wonder employee was coming to an end. A misunderstanding cost me my job. I'd left my clock card at Triona's bed sit, it was a plastic card with a bar code on, you would swipe in and out when entering and leaving the building. On this particular morning I was running late, I'd stayed on Madge's settee and didn't get much sleep. I arrived in work fifteen minutes late. I was about to go and tell the supervisor I'd lost my card when Triona stopped me and informed me she had it and had clocked me in at 6am. I said nothing and went about my work. I thought I'd got away with it. The shift was winding down and I was getting ready to go home. The supervisor shouted me over. She said I was to go upstairs to the manager's office. Someone had reported me, the manager had me on camera entering the factory at 6.15am but my clock card said I'd clocked in at 6am. I told him that someone must have found my card and clocked me in, thinking they were doing me a favour. The manager told me if I told him who clocked me in, I would get away with a written warning. How could I? I stuck to my story and after about ten minutes deliberation, my fate was sealed. To be fair to them, they didn't sack me. They just 'let me go.' This at least would ensure that I would get unemployment benefits. If you were sacked from a job, you were entitled to nothing.

That was the end of that. Golden Wonder closed the Widnes factory down over ten years ago. That hurt the town, a lot of people lost their jobs. A lot of my friends, I had some good memories from my time packing crisps.

It wasn't the last time I would see the factory. A police programme called 'Mersey Beat' used Widnes as it's setting and the old crispy was transformed into a mock up police station for the benefit of the show, that was surreal. My wife would follow the camera crew wherever they were filming, hoping our car would be used in one of the shots… it never was.

I was out of work and couldn't live the life style I'd become accustomed to, I started to do some work with my dad. Nothing permanent, two or three days a week. It was mainly demolition and collecting scrap, at least it was cash in hand. One particular job we had was collecting scrap metal from Astmoor Industrial Estate in nearby Runcorn. We would clear the yard every two weeks or so. Dad had a pick up truck, he would fill it to the brim, to get as much weight on the truck as we could. I'm pretty sure he never insured the truck. The Industrial estate was huge, row after row of small factories. There would be several sandwich vans littering the estate. There would be one less after my dad had his way.

As usual we stacked up the pick up and was driving down the estate heading for Widnes to weigh our scrap in. As we approached one of the sandwich vans, I noticed the open hatch of the van was sticking out into the road, I assumed dad had seen this and would move out a bit. He didn't, because our load was so high it hit the open hatch and spun the van full circle. Dad slammed on the brakes, we both jumped out. The two girls who were cooking in the van staggered out, they were shaking. Dad asked them if they were alright? I know I shouldn't but I had to turn around, to disguise my laughter. One of the girls had a rasher of bacon hanging from her head and a half cooked egg yolk running down her cheek. I was chuckling behind the pick up out of sight. Dad exchanged insurance details with the girls. I knew he had no insurance. On our next visit to the estate the van had gone, I asked one of the lads where they'd gone? He told me that the van had been burnt out nearly two weeks ago. Two days after dad had hit it. That meant dad was in the clear, they would only claim on the insurance for the fire and not from dad's 'insurance.' I looked over at him, he put his head down. I knew he was responsible for the van being burnt out and I think he knew I knew. We did a lot of work on the estate over the coming months, I don't know how. Dad never had any money, he still liked the horses too much. He'd go into a factory and tell them he had all the gear to do the job and they believed him. He could talk the talk. People would say he could sell sand to the Arabs. He would always say;

'Andrew, you go in there with clogs on and come out with brand new leather shoes.'

My income was practically none existent, as a result, my Landmark nights out were less and less. I would stay in most nights. Triona was still working and when she was on the two-ten shift I would stay at Madge's flat. We would sit up until the early hours playing the board game 'Trivial Pursuit.' Madge was quite intelligent. I also have always had a thirst for useless information, my head is full general knowledge stuff that's not really of any use, unless you happen to on a quiz show. For example, did you know that Humphrey Davy invented the miners safety lamp? Or Vacca is the Latin name for a cow? Did you want to know? As I said… useless.

Across from Madge's flat was Fiona Shaw's corner shop, Madge had a slate with her and would buy me four cans of beer every night. It wasn't the Landmark but it helped relieve the boredom. Fiona was in her late sixties, a plump woman with a slight blue rinse in her hair. This is something that always puzzled me, blue hair? At what point does a lady of a certain age decide to start wearing floral dresses and dye their hair a watery shade of blue. Is it a gradual process, or do they just wake up one morning, look in the mirror and think. 'Something isn't quite right, something's missing… blue hair and a knee length floral dress, looking good.'

I drank most nights and couldn't see it then but alcohol was starting to run my life, if I didn't have any I'd become cranky. Madge buying me beer most nights didn't help but I don't think she could ever envisage the road alcohol was leading me down.

Triona asked me if I wanted to move into the bed-sit with her. I talked it through with Madge and she reluctantly agreed that it wasn't practical for me to be living in a one bed flat with her. In any case the bed-sit was only a two-minute walk from Madge's flat and I'd see her most days anyway. Madge had kept me for the last five weeks and I think she was probably glad to see the back of me in many ways. The bed-sit wasn't bad, we had one room between the two of us, a television and video and it was clean. The only draw back was we had to share the kitchen and bathroom with two other people who lived there. You had to label all your food with your name so none of the other residents would eat it. This didn't always have the desired effect, quite often our food would go missing. I suspect it was the elder man who lived in the room upstairs. I confronted him but he denied it every time. One day I laid a trap. I left a tempting bar of chocolate in the fridge with 'Andy' clearly labelled on it. True to form, it went missing. What he didn't know was it was laxative chocolate. The old man couldn't get off the toilet for two days. He never touched our food again, though the smell in the bed-sit lingered for days.

Donna called at the bed-sit with two pieces of news. She was pregnant again. The second piece of news was more for my benefit. Peter was a sub-contractor and was working in Vauxhall Motors in Ellesmere Port. He'd got me a job as a 'Peggy.' A peggy was nothing more than a Goafer. I had to goafer this and had to goafer that. The money was good though, I'd earn twice as much as I did in the crispy and get a free meal every day. Part of my job was to go and get thirty fella's their bacon butties every morning, the sandwich would only cost £1.30 and they would always give me £1.50 and never asked for change, I'd end up with nearly six pounds change every day, it was a great job. I was soon upgraded to labourer and another lad was started to become the 'Peggy.' It was a promotion for me but I was gutted that my 'butty-run' had come to an end.

The site manager shouted me into his office one afternoon. He was in his fifties and spoke with a posh southern accent, I was like shit on his shoe and he spoke to me as such;

'Do you have a Fork Lift licence boy?' He asked, without lifting his head from his pretentious Daily Telegraph.

I told him I did indeed have a licence to drive a forklift. He told me I would become the new forklift driver as well as labourer. This was great news, I was getting promoted every other week, only problem was, I'd never driven a forklift truck in my life. Let alone had a licence. Two of the older guys took me in the warehouse on our dinner break and gave me a crash course on how to drive a forklift. 'Crash' being the operative word.

My first day as a bogus forklift driver began in earnest, it was going well. I'd unloaded one wagon. The lads were watching me through the window and every time I took something off the wagon, they would cheer. I've always hated people watching me do something, something usually goes wrong. This day was no exception. I'd taken my last load from the wagon to the ironic cheers coming from our cabin. I jumped off the truck and bowed in sarcastic acknowledgement. What I'd not done is put the forklift in neutral or put the hand brake on. The lads faces peering through the cabin window turned from smiles to panic, I wondered what was going on. I eventually turned around, the forklift was reversing on it's own and was heading straight for the supplies shed. I looked back towards the cabin, their faces were now motionless. I turned again and started sprinting after the runaway forklift. I was too late, the truck ploughed through the supplies shed. The boss must have heard the commotion, he rushed to his cabin door and stood with his head in his hands;

'My office…NOW!' He shouted down to me.

I thought I was going to lose my job. The older fella's told the boss that the forklift was faulty and I wasn't to know. I got away with it. We spent six months at Vauxhall Motors, before moving onto Ford Motors in Halewood, Liverpool. My luck was about to take a turn for the worse again.

I played football for the ICI Social club on Saturday mornings and although I no longer worked for Golden Wonder, I still played for them on a Sunday morning. I was insured against any accidents while playing for the ICI but had no insurance for the Golden Wonder.

We'd gone to the Landmark on the Saturday night and didn't get in until late. I heard a knock on the bed-sit front door. I looked at the clock, it was nine-thirty am.

'SHIT.' We had a match in less than half an hour. I threw on the clothes I had on from the night before and rushed to the door, it was Danny. We arrived at St Michael's playing field. The other team had not arrived yet, we didn't get changed into our kit yet in case they didn't show up. What happened next was sickening. Ryan passed the ball to me, it was less than waist height, I went to trap the ball in between my knees. I'd done it a thousand times without any problem, I heard a loud 'snap' and fell to the floor. I looked down at my right leg, it was deformed, I didn't know what had happened but I knew it wasn't good;

'I've broke my fucking leg.' I shouted to Danny and Ryan, they looked at me and laughed. They thought I was joking, then the pain kicked in. they stopped laughing and ran over to me. I recall one lad running away from me and throwing up on the side of the pitch. I passed out and can only remember being in an Ambulance with an oxygen mask on;

'Are you alright mate?' The ambulance man asked me.

I finally started to regain consciousness, the gas and air was amazing, I felt like I was floating. I looked down at my leg again, it was horrible. I lay back down and took another inhale on the mask. Out of nowhere a man's face was hovering over me. It was aunty Mavis's next door neighbour;

'I told you this would happen.' He said smugly.

'YOU'RE A FUCKING JINX.' I shouted, before passing out again.

I was taken to Whiston Hospital. I'd badly dislocated my right kneecap and damaged the surrounding ligaments. They kept me in for two days, such was the damage to my knee. I hate staying in hospital, the boredom and it's full of ill people. I stayed in hospital for concussion when I was

Madge

five years old. I cried every time Madge would have to leave after visiting. She took me to the hospital window and told me;

'Do you see that tree over there… I sleep under that every night so I'm never far away from you. You might not be able to see me but I'm there. If you get scared in the night, just look out of the window and I'll be able to see you.'

I would stand at the window, like she said, I never saw her but it comforted me thinking she was there.

I was scared this time, I was a contractor and if I didn't work, I didn't get paid. We'd already paid for our impending holiday to Yugoslavia but had no spending money. I left hospital in a full-length leg plaster. I went to see my boss at Halewood, he told me he'd pay me for a week but if I couldn't return to work after that, he would have to finish me up. He wasn't being cruel, that's the harsh realities of working as a contractor.

The week soon passed and I had to work for five weeks with my leg in plaster. I think the lads liked me and carried me as much as they could. That five-week period took its toll. My leg was never the same again and my best football days were definitely behind me.

I was looking forward to the holiday. My leg was still not quite right but was out of plaster. It was cheaper to go by coach, this had its drawbacks. The journey was over sixty hours long. I knew this before hand but was told you watch films and are entertained all the way through the long journey. I foolishly believed this, we did watch films… two films, again and again for nearly sixty hours. They weren't even good films. 'Twins.' Starring Dustin Hoffman and Tom Cruise, it wasn't bad first time around but after the fourth showing I wanted to go to the front of the coach and ram the videotape up the drivers arse. 'Masters Of The Universe.' Was the other film, need I say more?

The legroom was none existent. The coach wasn't fit for a trip to the Town centre, never mind a foreign country. My leg was starting to swell and I had to get off the coach every hour or so to exercise it. We travelled through France, Italy and Switzerland before arriving in Yugoslavia. Switzerland was beautiful and had amazing scenery. All we saw of France was the motorway and the odd service station, we stopped in one of these service stations for a well-earned 'stretch.' Ryan and I went to the toilet, as we stood there going about our business, I noticed something odd in the reflection of the chrome splash back surrounding the urinals. Sat directly behind me was an old lady at a table doing some knitting? I nudged Ryan and told him to look around. We both slowly turned around and sure enough, there she was. It became apparent that in France this is normal practice. The lady would insist on payment for the use of the toilet on the way out. This was alien to us but we washed our hands and handed the lady one franc, she shook her head, she wanted more. It cost the two of us ten francs to take a piss, I think we had the piss taken out of us in more ways than one.

The football World cup was already underway in Italy and the security at the border was doubled. They assumed because we were English we'd come for trouble, we must be thugs. We did coincide our holiday with the World Cup. Yugoslavia was right next to Italy and we naively thought we could pop over the border and catch a live game, not a chance. The Italian police took us off the coach and searched our bags, they found cigarettes that Ryan's girlfriend had bought at duty free. They thought they were drugs, or so they said. They confiscated them, there was not a lot we could do, we were in no position to argue. We just wanted to get to our final destination.

The rest of the journey was subdued. Our spirits were soon lifted when we approached the Yugoslav border, the Yugoslav police were a lot more helpful than the Italians. They checked our passports with a smile and wished us a good holiday.

We arrived in Porec; it was a beautiful old town on the banks of the Adriatic Sea. We were told to look out for pickpockets and prostitution, as the wages were so low here that people worked long hours for very little pay.

We were dropped off at what would be our apartment for the next two weeks. There were English flags everywhere, they obviously had the same idea as we did. I rang Madge to tell her I'd arrived in Yugoslavia. She told me to be careful, she'd read my stars and told me that all Capricorns were in danger of being caught in an avalanche;

'Mum.' I told her. 'I'm in one of the hottest countries in Europe, there's not much chance of an avalanche here.'

'Wait…wait… let me check.' She went on.

I could here paper shuffling over the telephone line, after about two minutes she came back on the phone;

'No, don't worry, I got it wrong, that was Sagittarius…but watch what you eat, you might need a dentist.'

Madge always read her stars and really believed what was written in them. As usual, they were wrong again. I never needed a dentist but it wouldn't be long before I found myself in a Yugoslav hospital and a prison cell.

The problems that soon ensued in this beautiful country were nothing to do with me. Although I do have a habit of finding trouble no matter where I go and Yugoslavia was just another unwanted feather in my cap.

CHAPTER FOURTEEN

Home Is Where The Heart Is.

This was the first time I'd ever been abroad, I didn't count Jersey or Ireland. Sure they were overseas but they were only 'baby abroad.' Yugoslavia was the real thing, a proper 'abroad.' I've always loved holidaying in England, the nearest thing to a foreign holiday would be Wales, I could handle that. I like the thought of being able to get home whenever I want because after a week on any holiday, I get bored and homesick. A week is just right, a fortnight is too long.

Porec was everything a foreign holiday should be, relaxing beaches, sun and alcohol. Even though I don't like beaches, I don't see the point of paying all that money just to read a book and fall asleep until your head fries. I don't like the sun either, it gives me migraines. So what was I doing in Yugoslavia? The alcohol… I could definitely live with that, and the fact the World Cup happened to coincide with our holiday was a bonus.

The worst thing I dislike about foreign holidays are the 'Brits abroad.' British people, for some reason feel the need to let everyone know where they're from. They adorn themselves in Union Jack shorts or T-shirts and are usually louder than anyone else, with the exception of The Scots. They're a scary race of people, they could beat you to a pulp at any minute and that's just the women! Then there's the Irish, a little more reserved than the Scot's but still let everyone know they're from the Emerald Isle. Even though not many of them actually live there anymore. I used to have that argument with Triona;

'If Ireland was the most beautiful country in the world, why live in England?'

There's the Welsh, you rarely see anyone walking around a foreign country with a pair of Welsh dragon shorts on. Maybe they don't need to let people know their heritage. They're happy with who they are and don't need to shout it from the rooftops. I think they're just smug bastards, they know they live in one of the most scenic countries in the world and only go on foreign holidays to tell everyone when they get home how shit other countries are compared to Wales.

Then finally there's Scouser's, wherever you go in the world I guarantee you'll bump into a scouser. You'll probably here them before you see them, they love that they come from Liverpool, the home of The Beatles. They're a proud race. I'm only surprised when Neil Armstrong landed on the moon and uttered the immortal lines;

'This is one small step for man...' That there wasn't a man in a Liverpool football shirt sat there with a can of Foster's in his hand shouting;

'ARIGHT MAYTE.'

The holiday didn't get off to the best start. Triona got food poisoning on the second day and had to stay in bed. I was the devoted boyfriend, I damped her head with a damp cloth and made sure she had plenty of water, then went to the bar with Ryan to watch the football. There was no point in both of us ruining our holiday, besides she had Patricia, Ryan's girlfriend to watch over her.

We'd already seen the qualifying rounds back in England and were at the quarter-final stage. We played Cameroon, a game we were expected to win but this was England. We were used to not winning but everyone was a bit more optimistic this time around. Bobby Robson was the manager and we had some great players, Paul Gascoigne was one of the best players in the world. The bar was full of Germans, Cameroon were 2-1 ahead with ten minutes to go. We were in real danger of going out of the World Cup again. The German's were loving it, they were singing their National Anthem at the top of their voices. Ryan and I sat nervously chomping away at our fingernails. Then with eight minutes to go Gary Lineker was fouled in the box. England had a penalty, I couldn't watch. Lineker stepped up to take the penalty and scored, it was 2-2 and it looked like extra time. Ryan ran over to the German contingent with his England shirt over his face;

'Not singing now you German bastards.' He screamed.

They were shouting something back at him. I did German at school and know some limited phrases but I don't think they were telling Ryan 'How to get to the Town Hall' or that 'The oranges were on the table.' England got another penalty in extra time. We won 3-2 and were in the semi finals of the World Cup, the closest I'd ever seen to us winning something. Who did we have to play…the fucking Germans!

We drank to the early hours, we were staggering up the small cobbled street singing in true 'Brit abroad' style when two German lads came up behind us. As they passed us one of them turned to Ryan and said;

'Wenker.'

'Who the fuck are you calling a wenker.' Ryan asked.

Their English was about as good as my German, I think they were trying to call Ryan a 'wanker,' Ryan ran up to the lads and hit one of them. He was like that, he'd hit first and ask questions later. Ryan was now fighting the two of them, I ran over to give Ryan a hand, I threw my first punch and missed, instead putting my left hand through a small window. The German lads started running, Ryan ran after them. I looked down at my hand, I'd cut the back of it, it was deep and there was blood everywhere. Before I had time to panic, I was surrounded by three Yugoslav police vans. These were not like police vans we get in England, they were small and looked like something we had in the sixties. They saw the blood, then put my good hand behind my back and threw me into the van. We arrived at a big white building, the paint was flaking off the exterior walls, it looked a depressing place. I thought it was the police station, instead it was the hospital. I was taken to a room with one chair in the middle, a doctor came in and looked at my hand, he said something to the police officer. Then looked back down at me in disgust. You couldn't blame him, I was just an English yob and he had to waste his valuable time stitching my hand up. They injected my hand to numb it but I could feel the needle going in and out, only for the fact I was still pissed I would have passed out.

After the doctor had finished I was put back in the van and taken to a smaller building. This was the police station, they threw me in a small cell. I was shitting myself, I'd heard about people being locked up in these Eastern European countries on the news and getting ten years. I looked at my watch and started to put a mark on the wall, like they do in the movies, just so I know how long I'd been there. After what seemed an eternity, I heard the cell door open. I looked at the wall, there were twelve marks on it. I'd been in there for twelve minutes…all right, hardly Nelson Mandella or Terry Waite but a frightening ordeal nonetheless.

The police had been to our apartment and got my passport from Triona. They sat me in a room and in walked one huge policeman. He looked me up and down, then took a seat across from me;

'So who has been a naughty boy?' His English was excellent. He went

Madge

on to tell me that I would be let off lightly this time but if he saw me again, they would throw me out of the country. I was relieved, he then drove me back to our apartment. I was half expecting the sort of reception hostages get after their release, girlfriends running up to them and throwing their arms around them, pleased to see them again, I opened the door and Triona stood there, looked at me and said;

'Soft shite.' Before running to the toilet to throw up.

My first real foreign holiday was turning into a nightmare, we'd only been there a week and I just wanted to go home. Ryan and I went out on our own most nights. Triona and Patricia preferred to stay in with a bottle of wine. We frequented the first bar we came across. It was a small bar and when they realised we were English the owner designated a waitress to our table. Every night we went in, the same waitress would serve us. She was a lovely girl and served on us hand and foot. She was unfortunate looking though, like most of the Yugoslav women we'd seen, she had facial hair and hairy legs. One particular night we gave her a tip, she refused and looked frightened. Before we could try and give her the money again, the owner came storming to our table and took the money off us. The waitress scurried off into the back, we could hear the owner shouting at her. We'd got her into trouble, we didn't know the protocol. The waitress was on a meagre wage and any tips they received went to the owner. The next night we went in the bar we didn't make the same mistake. This was the night when it came apparent how bad the wages were in Yugoslavia and the women were just packs of meat, used and abused. We sat at our usual table when a young girl walked in and sat directly across from us. She must have been about eighteen, she slid a card across the table. I picked the card up and read it, the girl was a prostitute and was asking us did we want 'fucky?' We politely refused and paid for her a drink before we left. As we got out the door there was a suspicious man hanging around outside the bar. Her pimp no doubt. We saw the same girl a couple of hours later walking down to the sea-front with two loud English guys, they'd obviously accepted her invitation for 'fucky.'

I felt sorry for the young girl and it preyed on my mind for some time after. I could tell by the look on her face that she was embarrassed to be doing what she was doing but had little choice. I also felt bad just for being in this beautiful country. Here we were throwing our money about like it was confetti, these poor bastards were willing to sell their soul for the price of a meal. I'd seen enough, I was ready to go home.

We thought the holiday was for fourteen days, including the travel. We went to the tour office and asked what time the coach would be leaving. They informed us that we had three days left of our holiday. Three days return travel and fourteen days in Porec, seventeen days in total. We were gutted, we were all due back in work the following Monday. That wasn't the biggest problem, because we'd got the duration of the holiday completely wrong, we'd be travelling home when England were playing West Germany in the semi-finals of the World Cup and we would miss the game. Ryan and I were devastated, we tried everything to persuade the travel agents to let us go on an earlier coach, but their wasn't one, we'd have to wait. It was a good thing that the girls had a bit more common sense than us, they'd saved a lot of their money. Ryan and I had blown most of ours thinking we were going home the following day.

The four of us went shopping on the last day to buy presents for everyone back home at the local market. I've always loved markets and this one was no exception. It wasn't like the markets you get in England, children would follow you around trying to sell you their hand crafted wooden animals, stall holders would be shouting you over;

'Hey, English… come and buy from me.'

I assume they knew we were English because of the British Bulldog tattoo Ryan had on his arm. Or perhaps it was the Union Jack shorts and socks I was wearing, despite vowing never to indulge in any such behaviour. I'd become a Brit Abroad. Or to give it another name… a dickhead! All through the holiday they would ask if we were English, they loved us. They hated the German's and wouldn't serve them in a lot of the bars and cafés. They'd still not forgiven them for the atrocities of the Second World War. Looking back, I think that's why I got off so lightly with the police, they didn't mind anyone who was trying to hit a German.

This was unlike any market I'd ever been to. At home, you see what you want and buy it. Here you are expected to haggle, I saw a wooden carved chess set. My dad loved chess and this was an ideal present. I picked it up and asked how much, it was the equivalent of five pounds in English money. I paid the money and took the chess board;

'What are you doing? You've got to haggle with them, I would have got that for three quid.' Ryan told me. He'd been abroad before and knew how to buy off these foreigners. He wanted a chessboard for his dad and told me to watch and learn. We went to another stall further up the street and Ryan went to work. He'd seen an identical board to the one I'd just bought.

'How much?' Ryan asked the stallholder.

He told him a price. Ryan looked around at me and gave me a wink as if to say 'Watch and learn.' The stallholder was dropping his price and I was slightly impressed. They eventually agreed on a price, shook hands and completed the transaction.

'How much did you get it for then?' I asked the now smug looking Ryan. We worked it out and converted it into English money. Ryan's face turned from smug to embarrassed;

'How much?' Patricia asked again.

'Six fucking pounds.' Was his mumbled reply.

We all started laughing hysterically. For all of Ryan's haggling he'd still paid one pound more than I did for my chessboard. As if he didn't look stupid enough, I offered to swap my identical chessboard that I paid five pounds for, for the one he just paid six pounds for. He thought about it for a few minutes and accepted my swap, the smug look reappeared on his face. He turned around to Patricia, nodded in my direction and said;

'Thick fuck, he's just lost a pound on that.'

We'd bought everything we needed, I bought Madge two hand carved male and female ivory statues. I didn't know what else to buy, I've always been bad at buying presents for people.

Last Christmas my wife entrusted me to buy the family's Christmas presents as she was working and didn't have the time. A decision she later regretted. I bought everyone a paper shredder, with the exception of her mum. I bought her a set of hand warmers. Luckily for me they all found it quite funny. My wife didn't and banned me from doing any shopping for presents again. You may be forgiven for thinking I'd done it on purpose, so I wouldn't have to do the shopping again. But you'd be wrong, I genuinely thought every home should have a paper shredder and her mum has bad circulation in her hands. They were all practical presents.

We had one night left in Porec. We were all relieved to be going home the next day. We still couldn't believe we were going to miss the England game but at least we'd be home for the final if we beat the German's. We had about fifty pounds left in Yugoslav money and decided to have one last blow out. There was no point in taking any of the money home, because of the exchange rate it was worthless.

The four of us got ready and headed for the usual bar, we had a few drinks and was planning to go on to another bar. As we were about to leave the owner came over and shook our hands and gave us a drink on the house. Ryan and I kept the owner talking about football, he wished England would win against 'those bastard German's.' Whilst we had his attention the girls sneaked over to the waitress who'd looked after us and slipped a wad of notes into her hand. She looked over at the owner but he was too busy talking to us to notice. The waitress smiled and ran into the back room. We'd given her the equivalent of a month's wages, nothing to us but a lot to her.

We went from bar to bar and had the best night of the holiday. We arrived back at the apartment at three in the morning. The next morning the hangover had kicked in. The coach came and picked us up and we slept for most of the first day. We passed through Italy without any delay, they didn't care now we were going home they wanted rid of the English scum.

The second day on the coach is something I'll never forget. England were due to start the semi-final match, we all had radios and were frantically trying to tune into the match. We were going through the French Alps and had little chance of a reception. I threw the radio to the ground in temper, then a young lad ran up the stairs and told us the driver had got the game on his radio. We ran down to the front of the coach and sure enough he had the game on, but it was in French. We couldn't understand a word of it, after ten minutes we decided to go back to our seats. This was worse than not watching it. The driver said he could speak French and would keep us all informed. He told us the game was going into extra time, it was horrible. He then told us it was going to penalties. We all waited with baited breath. After what seemed forever, the Polish driver who could apparently speak French announced over the tannoy;

'Congratulations... England are in the World Cup final.'

The whole coach went berserk, we were hugging everyone in sight. The driver stopped and got a crate of beer out of the boot and handed them around, we celebrated well into the night. We arrived at Calais the next morning still buzzing from the previous nights celebrations. Our celebrations were soon to be brought down to earth with a bang. There were a coach load of German's coming off the ferry, when they saw the English flags hung from our coach windows they started shouting and cheering at us. We were confused, why would they be acting like that, we'd just knocked them out of the World Cup. I looked at Ryan and immediately ran to find a newspaper. I didn't have to be able to speak French to read the result. The fluent French speaking Polish driver had got it wrong. We were beaten on penalties by West Germany. We were gutted,

Madge

the coach driver made a quick exit when he realised his mistake. He was a lucky man, I think he would have been hung drawn and quartered had we got our hands on him.

Yet again we were on a downer, it was made even worse when we were told we would have to wait a few hours before we could cross the English Channel as the weather was too bad. After two and a half hours they eventually let us on the boat. The water was really choppy and the winds were high. As usual the first thing I did was head for the bar. I could tell by the look on people's faces that they were apprehensive, the boat was going up and down like a roller coaster, my stomach was turning. I really thought we were going to turn over. Even Triona and Patricia looked worried and they'd crossed the Irish sea, one of the most tempestuous sea's in the world, on several occasions. People were laughing and joking nervously. I was starting to panic and kept on drinking to ease my nerves. I looked over to the other side of the boat and seen a priest holding some Rosary Beads and praying;

'Fuck me, if we're going down, I'm going down pissed.' I said to Ryan.

He agreed and we stumbled over to the bar for another drink. The bottles and glasses were literally falling out of their optics and smashing on the floor. The bar staff were still trying to serve with their best customer relations smile;

'Is this normal?' Ryan asked the barman while clinging to the bar, doing his best to stay on his feet.

'No sir, this is the worst I've ever experienced.'

He could of lied, reassured us. The takings in the bar must have been the biggest they'd ever taken. Everyone was ordering drinks like it was their last one. I clung on to my drink and headed for the door near the lifeboats, I've seen the film 'Titanic.' All that was going through my mind was the ambulance man at aunty Mavis's party. He got the football injury right and he said I would have a bad crossing by boat. He never said I would die though... but he wouldn't say that would he? That would have put a dampener on the party.

The Captain's voice came over the loud speaker and told us we were through the worst and that the weather was taking a turn for the better. Everyone looked relieved and headed for the bar again. I wasn't going anywhere, I stayed by the lifeboats until I saw those famous White Cliffs appearing through the mist.

That was the last time I ever went on a 'proper' foreign holiday. I swore to myself that I'd keep my feet firmly on English soil from now on. We were due to go back to Ireland later that year but that didn't count, that was a 'baby' abroad.

No, I would never grace these foreign lands again, you can go anywhere in the world but in my humble opinion… home is definitely where the heart is!

CHAPTER FIFTEEN

Playing Away.

It was some months later that the news of Civil War had broken out in Yugoslavia. The horrendous pictures were on the news and in the newspapers for all to see. It felt surreal that we were there not so long ago, I wasn't even sure what the war was about but I bet religion had something to do with it. All I could think about was that poor waitress who treated us like royalty, what were the implications for her? Was she still alive? I don't know. What I did know was, that beautiful country would never be the same again.

In contrast, my life was working out quite well. I was working twelve-hour shifts at Ford Motors but the money was good. There was an irony, after me swearing I'd never step foot on foreign soil again we were told that when we'd finished work in Fords we would be heading to another car plant… in Germany. This was six months down the line and I would cross that bridge when I came to it.

I moved back into Madge's flat for a week, the bed sit was getting redecorated, Triona stayed there, it was okay for one person but too cramped for two. I would spend a few hours there then go back to the flat to sleep. One Friday evening I'd been in the Landmark nightclub with Ronnie, Triona had gone to a different club. It was after two in the morning, I decided to go to the bed sit and stay with Triona so as not to wake Madge up. Triona wasn't expecting me that night, that was evident. I let myself in the bed-sit and heard voices coming from the parlour. It was Patricia with another Irish friend of hers;

'Andy, what are ye doing here?' She said.

'I live here…where's Triona?'

'I thought ye were staying with yer mam for a week?' She sounded flustered.

She went on to tell me that Triona was still at the kebab shop with friends and she'd go and get her. I told her I would walk down and meet her. After walking one or so hundred yards I saw Triona walking up the road linking some guy. They were laughing and joking, I stood in a bus stop they were approaching. As they got closer I recognised the guy. His name was John and he worked at the Crispy, he was also married to a girl who was on the other shift at the Crispy. I let them walk past the bus stop, they were still unaware I was there. I stepped out and said;

'Enjoying yourself?'

They both stopped dead in their tracks, they weren't laughing now. They turned around and I don't know who's face drained of colour the most;

'I can exp…' John said as he walked towards me.

Without saying a word, I punched him square in the jaw and said;

'Explain that to your wife.'

Triona didn't say a word, she just looked at me. I smiled at her and calmly said;

'He's all yours.' Before walking away.

Two things pissed me off about that night. One, John was an ugly bastard and two, I had plenty of offers in the Landmark but said no because I was with someone.

I was walking along Milton Road towards Madge's flat when I heard Triona running after me crying, telling me nothing was going on and they were just mates. I never believed her for a minute. We ended up talking and both stayed at the flat that night. I was sat in the chair watching 'Big Break' a game show Madge had previously taped on her new VHS recorder, it was about four in the morning. Triona was asleep on the settee, she got up and said she was going to the toilet, I noticed she'd turned the wrong way and was heading for Madge's bedroom. Under normal circumstances I would have stopped her, but after what had happened with ugly John I thought I'd just sit back and see what happens. After two minutes or so I heard Madge scream;

'What the hell… Who's that?' Triona, still drunk had climbed into bed with Madge. I then heard Triona let out a scream and run for the door, because it was pitch black she opened the wardrobe door, thinking it was the bedroom door and ran inside. By now it was like something out of Monty Python, I was in hysterics in the living room. Madge turned the bedroom light on and saw Triona stuck in her wardrobe, fighting her way through her fake fur coats.

Madge had a warped sense of humour and found the incident hilarious the next morning. Triona made a quick exit before Madge got up, she stood at the bottom of the stairs and before she opened the door, she looked up at me and said;

'You're gonna' get me back for last night aren't ye?'

'For getting in bed with my mum?' I replied.

'For the, the… John thing.' She said bowing her head.

I laughed and walked down the stairs towards her, put my arm on her shoulder. I'd stopped laughing now and looked at her with my best Marlon Brando look, mean and moody and whispered;

'You bet your fucking life I am.'

I never quite trusted her after that night. I stayed with her, she was a means to an end. As for John, I saw him with his wife in the Market. His face was a picture, he must have thought I was going to say something to her, but that's never been my way. I'm sure she would find out what a prick he was without my help. I did enjoy the look on his face every time I saw him after though.

John wasn't the only person in the Crispy who was having extra-marital affairs, it was like a den of iniquity. Too many men and women working in the same environment. That factory was the cause of many a divorce over the years. Not every one was at it but I'd say about fifty per cent of our shift was having it away behind their spouses back. The night shift was allegedly the worse, rumour had it they would be going at it like rabbits in the spud bashing plant when they were supposed to be working, like I said… 'Allegedly.'

I decided to stay at Madge's flat for another week. The bed-sit was ready for me to move back in but I was making Triona suffer for her own attempted infidelity. She said nothing happened with ugly John, I'm sure it didn't but that was only because I caught them. I was more concerned at what would have happened had I not have been there.

News of our Donna giving birth to her second child spread around the family, she'd had another girl. Madge and I went to the hospital. We walked in the maternity ward and Donna was crying;

'What's the matter? Is everything alright with the baby?' Madge asked.

'No… she's… she's..' Donna couldn't get her words out, she was too upset.

'She's what?' Madge asked fearing there was something badly wrong with the baby.

'She's... ugly.' Donna sobbed.

Madge looked into the crib at the side of Donna's bed and assured Donna that baby Jenna was beautiful. Donna asked me to look at her and tell her what I thought. I walked over and took a long look at the baby.

'What do you think?' Donna asked.

My niece lay there with a mop of ginger hair and with an uncanny likeness to Winstone Churchill. Donna asked me again;

'What do you think Andrew?'

I thought for a minute, I wanted to be diplomatic and assure Donna that she was beautiful, then for some unknown reason these words came out;

'Yep, sis… that's one ugly kid.'

Donna started crying again, Madge gave me a look that could kill. I've always had a habit of saying what I'm actually thinking, not on purpose, it just comes out. Jenna turned out to be a beautiful little girl, you were only ugly for a bit love.

I recall being in a pub with my dad, he started a singsong. Everyone had a turn. It was a good night until I started to think out loud. I noticed a coloured guy stood at the end of the bar, he was enjoying the entertainment but wasn't singing;

'Come on mate, give us a song.' I said.

'No, I can't sing a note mate.' He replied. To which I said;

'You must be able to sing… you're black!'

Dad spit his pint out, the pub fell silent. There were a few coloured people in the bar that night, they all stopped and looked at me. I was half expecting Tumble Weed to roll across the floor. I meant it as a compliment. I thought I was going to get lynched. Then the guy I'd just insulted walked over to me and put his arm on my shoulder and started to sing *'Sitting On The Dock Of The Bay.'* By the legendary Otis Redding, we did a duet and the situation had been defused. He actually had a voice like a bird, a Kestrel. He was right, he couldn't sing a note.

We'd arranged to have a get together in Leggies to 'Whet the babies head.' It was a good excuse for a party. Bryan and Vin were all there.

Dad turned up with a new woman on his arm, Shirley. She seemed nice enough, he sat her in the corner and went onto to do his Don Corleone routine, buying everyone who walked in a drink and telling them he was a granddad again. The night was going off with a bang. Vin told me there was a party he knew of and did I want to go for a bit of after hours drinking. I had no work the next day so I agreed. I was starting to enjoy my semi-single life.

We headed off towards the estate we know as 'The Bronx.' I felt safe enough, Vin was a bit of a rogue and was well known in the area. We arrived at the house where the party was being held. There were several people stood outside with drinks in their hands but I couldn't here any music. I wondered why Vin had pinched some flowers from a neighbouring garden. We walked into the kitchen and got ourselves a drink and Vin went over to an old lady sat in the corner and handed her the flowers before kissing her on the cheek.

'She's in the parlour love.' The old lady said to Vin.

This was one of the strangest parties I'd ever been to. Vin nodded to me telling me to follow him to the parlour. There was an over whelming sickly smell of flowers. We entered the parlour and in the corner lay an opened coffin with a body of a woman in it. He'd brought me to a fucking wake, what's more I didn't even know the woman. Vin went and shook the family members hands and went over to the coffin. He bent down and kissed the woman's fore head, he even managed to squeeze out a tear. He shouted me over and said;

'Kiss her head.'

'Fuck off, she's dead.' I whispered.

The family members were looking at me. So out of respect I bent over and kissed this dead woman's fore head.

'There you go, now go and get another drink… you're practically family.' Vin assured me.

People started to sing the sombre Irish songs that I knew only too well. I don't think they were Irish at all but they always go down well at a wake. After a couple of Whiskey's I decided to pay my own tribute to… I asked Vin what the dead woman's name was. He said he thought it might be Julie. I sang *A Bunch Of Thyme* a classic Irish song and incidentally one of Madge's favourites. It went down well, people were actually hugging me and consoling me for my loss. It turned out to be one of the best parties I'd ever been to.

I was enjoying staying with Madge again. Just like the old days we would sit up into the early hours and she would tell me stories of her youth. The time when she and dad were first married and happy. Dad's first job was on the railway, he was a fireman. Not the sort of firemen we associate with now, a fireman's job on the railway was to shovel coal in the furnace to keep the engine going. She told me how dad woke her up in the middle of the night;

'He was like a little boy on Christmas morning.' She told me.

He took her to the railway sidings in West Bank, they stopped and dad said to Madge;

'There she is, isn't she beautiful?'

It was the 'Flying Scotsman,' Madge wasn't impressed, she'd been dragged out of bed in the middle of the night to look at a train! Like all those years ago I could see the glint in her eye as she was relating the story to me. I could sit for hours and just listen to people telling stories. I love the look on their faces as they relate them, you can see they're back in that time, a time when they were happy. Just like Madge, when the story ends they give a smile and come back to earth with a bump. Their eyes die again. I asked Madge for the first time, did she still miss gran Holland;

'Every day.' Was her quiet response.

All this got me thinking about my own life. Did I really want to spend my life with a girl who I didn't really love or trust? Did she want to spend it with me? I was going with girls behind her back at every given opportunity. It was hardly a perfect relationship. Then Triona pulled a masterstroke. She called at Madge's flat and asked me to take a walk with her, we walked for about five minutes and she stopped and grabbed my arm. We were stood in front of a furniture shop in Alforde Street, directly across from Widnes Market;

'It's ours if we want it.' She said excitingly.

There was an old-fashioned three-piece suite in the shop window, I was confused and said;

'You've brought me here to look at an old settee?'

She hadn't, she'd secured the rental of the flat above the shop and asked if we could start again in our own place. She had the keys and we went inside, it was a nice flat. She knew I always wanted a place of my own, somewhere I could call mine instead of having to move from house to house. I told her I would think about it. We went back to the bed-sit and

I told her everything. She cried but said she really wanted to start again and put the past behind us.

We decided to give it another go. I was on good money and went to Ikea and bought all new furniture for the flat. I didn't know it then but it turns out Triona had a hidden agenda of her own. She invited her mum and dad over from Ireland to stay with us for a week. Once again I had to stay with Madge, Triona had to pretend the flat was hers as her dad didn't agree with cavorting before marriage, him being a 'good' Catholic and all. Her mum was a bit more liberal and told me she knew we were living together;

'Just don't tell Da.' She said with a wink.

She got on with Madge like a house on fire and invited her over to Ireland the coming Christmas. I was approaching my Twenty-First birthday and could think of nothing better than to have Madge come to Ireland with us. Madge was excited, she'd never left these shores before and was telling everyone she was going abroad for Christmas. She would ask people what they were doing for Christmas knowing they would ask her back;

'I'm going abroad.' She would say with a daft smile.

I noticed Triona's dad never went to church once while he was over here. He said he liked to stay true to his own parish in Clonaslee. That week was like an Irish week, we must have visited every Irish in pub in the region. Why bother coming to England I thought. Surely the reason for going to another country is to sample their culture, not bring your own with you. They had a good time but I couldn't wait for them to go home. I was sick of the sight of Guinness and wanted to get back in my own flat.

Madge had been good to me while I was out of work, so every week I would slip her some money to go to the Bingo. Triona didn't like me doing this and it caused several arguments. I told her I'd stop. I didn't, I just told Madge not to tell her. I felt quite bad lying to Triona but I wasn't going to see my mum go without. I had a physio appointment and had to take the day off work, I heard the post come through the letterbox. There was a letter from Triona's mum, I put it on the mantle-piece until she got home from work. Normally she would give me the letters to read, on this occasion she read it and put it into her pocket. I asked why she didn't give it me to read.

'Just the same old boring stuff from home.' She replied.

My suspicions became aroused, I wondered what was in the letter that she didn't want me to read. I said nothing. Later that night when she was in the bath I took the letter out of her pocket and read it. Like she said just boring stuff from home, until I got to the P.S bit at the bottom of the letter, it read;

P.S,

Thank-you for the new video recorder and telephone.

I couldn't believe it, she was going mad at me because I was giving Madge twenty pounds to go to the bingo. Yet she'd paid for a phone to be installed for her mum and bought them a new video behind my back. I was furious, she got out of the bath and saw me with the letter in my hand. She didn't know what to say. I wouldn't have minded her doing that for her mum and dad had she not been so against me giving my own mother a few bob here and there. It caused a massive argument and I stormed out and went to the pub.

I arrived home from work the next day, she was full of apologies and even had my tea ready… Irish Stew, what else. I told her it didn't matter and to forget about it. I was about to put my first mouthful of food into my mouth, Triona turned to go into the kitchen when I asked;

'I'm going shopping tomorrow after work, you want to come?'

She looked excited, what woman doesn't like to go shopping. She immediately agreed;

'Yes I'd love to, what are we going for?'

'A new telly for my mum.' I said, with the spoon full of food poised at my open mouth.

'Is that okay?' I asked.

She forced a ridiculous false smile and through gritted teeth she stood in the doorway and said;

'I can't wait.'

I continued to eat my tea with a smug smile on my face. I heard the dishes clattering in the kitchen, she was less than happy but could do nothing about it.

My leg was playing up, it was giving me problems. It would swell up and at times I couldn't walk on it. Working in a full-length plaster after my injury was taking its toll. The doctor sent me to see an Orthopaedic specialist, he told me that if I carried on working and didn't rest it for three months I would be in danger of losing it. I didn't know what to do, I couldn't afford to lose my job. I said nothing to anyone and carried on working. I did stop playing football and started to wear an orthopaedic stocking, that helped but the thought of losing my leg was a constant worry.

Christmas and my Twenty-First birthday were fast approaching. Madge was looking forward to her 'foreign' holiday and I put all negative thoughts to the back of my mind until after the holidays. This is where Triona's new agenda came into play. She kept saying she was homesick and would love to go back to Ireland to live. At first I had no intention of moving to Ireland but given my current circumstances it might be the perfect opportunity to rest. I told her we'd use this holiday as a dry run, to see how it went. A holidays one thing but living there is something different altogether. I told Triona not to tell anyone what we were thinking of doing… Especially Madge.

Madge had never travelled on a boat or plane before, she was apprehensive and somewhat relieved when we told her we would be sailing;

'That's the less of two evils.' She said.

Madge was waiting at the bottom of the stairs with her coat on and her suitcases either side of her. She was like a kid going on her first trip to Chester Zoo. I got out of Ryan's car and put her cases in the back;

'Are you ready for this mum?' I asked.

With a grin as wide as the Mersey Tunnel, she looked at me and said;

'Are you sure you want me there son?'

I smiled, gave her a kiss on the cheek and said;

'I couldn't think of anyone better mum.'

CHAPTER SIXTEEN

ON THE FENCE.

The closer we got to the ferry terminal at Liverpool, the quieter Madge was becoming. I could tell she was nervous she was clicking her nails. She always did that when she was nervous. I reassured her that the crossing would be fine. The first thing I did when we got on the boat was to buy her a stiff drink. It calmed her down a bit. She wouldn't take her coat off, I asked her why, she said;

'In case the boat sinks and I end up in the water, it will keep me that bit warmer.'

We all laughed. The crossing of the Irish Sea was one of the smoothest I'd ever experienced. The sea gods must have been on Madge's side that night.

Ryan was driving his mark II Escort, at least we didn't have to take the long coach journey this time. We arrived in the village to a small welcome committee, Triona's mum and dad were there along with Paddy Kelly. Even Sean O'Brien, the football captain was there, his little face was beaming at the thought of me re-enacting the previous years exploits against the neighbouring village. News hadn't filtered through that I'd had a bad injury since I was last there and wouldn't be able to play this year. His bubble was well and truly burst, he walked off with his head down scuttering to himself, I shouted him back and said;

'Sean, maybe I can come on as a sub.'

'Fecking yes.' He said, before running back to the Post Office where he worked as Postmaster.

Triona looked at me and reminded me about my leg, if only she knew the full extent and what the specialist had told me. After last year they were expecting a lot from me. I couldn't let my fans down.

We all ploughed into Paddy's bar and had a few introductory drinks. Madge had never seen anything like this. I reminded her not to talk about politics or religion, especially Maggie Thatcher. She pulled her fingers across her mouth indicating she'd keep it zipped. She meant it, but I knew this could be a bit of a problem when she'd had a few to drink, she didn't drink that much any more but I was still a little apprehensive. She was a stern patriarch and just like the Argentinean Corned Beef incident, she would stand toe to toe with anyone who slagged off 'her' country. Triona's mum grabbed Madge by the arm and said;

'Come on Madge, I'll show ye 'round the village.'

Ryan leaned over to me and whispered;

'That should take about three minutes then.'

I was glad Ryan was in his car, Madge would never be able to manage the 'short walk' to the house. She could barely walk to the shop without having to stop for breath. They came back from the tour, Madge had been to the butchers and bought half a pound of White Pudding. She commented that the world was going mad;

'I can't believe you can't even call a pudding black without being racist.'

Of course White Pudding was so called because… it was white as opposed to Black Pudding she was accustomed to back home. It is an Irish dish and has a lovely taste. I tried for years to get it in England, it's only in recent years that it's become widely available.

Triona's dad John threw back his Guinness, let out his customary burp and said something to Ryan and I, I say he said something but to be honest his we couldn't understand a word he was saying. Until we were pissed, then we were fluent. Patricia translated what her dad was saying;

'He wants to show you something.'

We finished our drink and followed John, we seemed to be walking for ages. We eventually stopped in a field. In front of us lay a dead cow;

'Whartyatinkodatden?' He said.

I think he was saying 'What do you think of that then?' Ryan looked at the dead cow then up at me. I was confused, I didn't know why we were here. Did he want us to do something with it? I stood with my hands on my hips and said the first thing that came to mind;

'How did he die?'

John started laughing and waving his finger before heading back for the bar. Ryan and I stood looking at each other in bemusement. I'm sure there was a lesson to be learned, what it was is beyond me. We got back to the bar and John informed everyone that we'd just seen our first dead cow. They all raised their glasses, I was going to ask the significance of seeing you first dead cow but I just left it, I was scared to ask.

After that surreal afternoon we headed for the house. Madge was to sleep in the bed I previously slept in and I would have to sleep at the foot of her bed on the floor. I hardly got any sleep, it was freezing and when I eventually did get to sleep I was woken up at the crack of dawn by a cockerel outside the bedroom window. Three mornings on the run that little bastard woke me up. I happened to mention the cockerel to John and good enough it stopped. I assumed he'd moved it. I thanked him for moving the cockerel and told him I was sleeping much better now.

'Oh he didn't move it, ye ate it on Sunday.' Triona's mum so matter-of-factly informed me.

I felt slightly guilty that I'd condemned the little bastard to its death. It tasted really good though. That was the same Sunday that Madge really surprised me. She'd agreed to go to church with the rest of them. I overheard her tell Bridy that she regularly goes to church back home. I couldn't believe my ears, the only time she attended church was weddings, funerals and christenings. I popped my head around the door and looked at Madge, she looked back at me and didn't flinch. She even brought me into her catalogue of lies;

'Don't I Andrew? Go to church a lot?'

'Like your life depended on it mum.' I replied with an air of sarcasm.

Madge attended church and told everyone she really enjoyed the service, I could tell she hated it, she later confirmed my suspicions when I asked her how it went;

'It would be better if the priest did a bingo.' She laughed.

I was still pondering about moving here for good the following year, what would I do? I need to rest my leg, for that purpose it would be ideal, if I were writing a book like I am now… perfect. But day in day out of doing nothing would drive me insane. Triona was hell bent on moving back to Ireland and I understood that. It became harder and harder for her to leave after every visit. John made extra money by chopping wood and selling it to the locals, I suppose I could do that, it's hardly a living though.

I was thinking too much, I put any idea of living here out of my mind and concentrate on the rest of the holiday. We were all getting ready for the

Madge

big night out, the bar was hosting a talent contest. At least it was different from Irish music nights, or so I thought. This was exactly the same as Irish music nights but with people who couldn't sing and definitely had no talent. Paddy O'Leary, the all-singing, all dancing pig farmer from Toolabolach Lane was announced. With an introduction like that he had to be good. He wasn't! He sang *'Come Down From The Mountain Katy Daly'* while playing a mouth organ and doing an Irish Jig. Next up were the Conlan siblings, a brother and sister aged about twelve and thirteen respectively. The boy sang *'Walking In The Air,'* He wasn't bad but all his sister did was a weird ballet dance behind him. The poor girl probably wasn't blessed with her brother's tonsils so her mum and dad just through a leotard on her and said;

'Ye can't sing for shite, but ye dance like an angel… now just stand behind yer brother.'

The more I drank the better the night was going, talent shows should be bad. They are like Karaoke. Nobody wants to see a good singer, we want to see people make a show of themselves. I want to see people who are that bad, they're good.

Quite recently I've started to watch a programme called 'Dancing On Ice.' Not because I like it, I don't. but there's a contestant on it with a false leg. Please don't tell me I'm the only person watching and waiting for the moment the contestant goes in one direction while her dance partner is skating off in the other direction holding her false leg, it would be quality television.

The last person on stage that night was a local celebrity, Sioban had won the talent show three years on the run. She took it seriously, it was said that she wouldn't speak to anyone for half an hour before she was due to perform, so she didn't strain her vocal chords. She sang *Nessun Dorma* and was head and shoulders better than everyone else and was in line for her fourth consecutive win. The first prize was all but hers, a Ten-pound meat hamper from Serle the Butcher and two weeks worth of complimentary stamps donated by the Post Office. But this year was full of controversy. The Conlan siblings were the surprise winners, it helped that their older sister and their uncle were two of the three man-judging panel. Sioban stormed out of the bar and vowed never to enter the competition again. She even turned down the second prize, a voucher to the value of five pounds to be spent in the local chip-shop.

The Garda had been told to stop the stay behind drinking. We had to be out of the bar by eleven pm. We carried on the party at JD's house, he was John and Bridie's next-door neighbour. Although his house was some five hundred yards from their house it was the closest. JD was a real character and a lovely man. He stood about six foot four and was big set. He wasn't the brightest lamp in the street. He'd not long finished a two-year prison sentence. I asked what he'd done to get two years, he said he was lucky. He thought he'd get five years for what he did.

He went on to tell me that where he used to live in Dublin, he owned seven cows. Two of which had been poisoned, he suspected the neighbouring farmer. The feud between them went on for some months, JD finally snapped when he found three of his chickens had been strangled. He waited until nightfall and went to his neighbouring farmers field and shot five of his cows. It turns out that because it was pitch black he took a wrong turn and ended back in his own field and shot his own cows. He got two years for the wrongful use of a firearm. The judge told him had it not have been his own cows he shot, he would have got five years.

'So ye see, I was lucky really.' He smiled.

'Fucking stupid.' I thought, remind me not to mess with JD's cows or chickens.

I was keeping my eye on Madge, she was hardly drinking and was seeming to have a really good time. That's the one thing I will say about the people of Clonaslee, they made you feel like one of their own and Madge was no exception, she fitted straight in.

The next day was the 'Big Match,' there were about fifty people there watching in anticipation. I was a substitute, Ryan started the game and was playing well. The match was evenly poised at 0-0. My heart wanted to play but my head and leg didn't want any of it, I was asked did I want to go on at half-time, I told them they were doing well without me and could win. With twenty minutes to go the worst thing happened, the other team scored. Our fans were having a go at our manager to put me on. The inevitable happened, I was told to get my tracksuit bottoms off. I was going on. I could hear the buzz in the crowd, they thought I was going to repeat the heroics of last year. To be honest, apart from my leg my fitness wasn't there. I'd not trained in months and the constant intake of alcohol had caused me to put on a bit of weight.

The ball was immediately passed back to me, I laid it off to Ryan immediately. I couldn't risk another tackle like the one I got the previous year, Ryan could take all the credit this year. He took on two players and crossed the ball in the box, it was a great cross to young Liam Murphy. He was about to shoot when he was fouled from behind, we won a penalty. Liam took the penalty and scored, it was 1-1. The game finished that way and young Liam was the toast of the village that year. He deserved it, he was a great little player. As for me, I was just glad to play for twenty minutes without getting injured. I did nothing spectacular, I couldn't but I think I got away with it.

For days after my leg swelled up and I was in agony. It was then the realisation hit me. I would never be able to play football again, Jesus if I was struggling in a village team I wouldn't stand a chance back home. Don't get me wrong, Alex Ferguson wasn't ever going to knock on my door but I've loved playing football all my life and I knew I would miss playing. If someone has a passion for knitting and loses all their fingers, what would they do?

The 22nd of December soon arrived. It was my Twenty-First birthday, unlike my Eighteenth this was anything but quiet. We were going to celebrate it in 'grand style.' We had a party in Paddy Kelly's bar, where else! And the entertainment… Irish music. It was a good enough night, pretty much the same as all the other nights in Paddy's bar. But I appreciated that it had been laid on in honour of my birthday. Paddy locked the front doors so we could indulge in some after hours drinking. The Garda were on the look out and were determined to stop any late night drinking. That surprised me because it was usually the Garda who were drinking after hours. The village had a new sergeant 'from the big city' no less, Dublin and he was hell bent on stamping his authority in the village;

'Fecking big city shite, coming to our village an' tellin' me what to do in my own bar.' Paddy was ranting.

'If he comes to my door I'll tell him to feck off.' He continued.

The whole bar raised their glasses in acknowledgement of his speech and said they would all stand defiant against the man from the big city.

The 'Fight them on the beaches' speech was interrupted by a loud knock on the door;

'This is the Garda, are ye still serving alcohol in that there bar Paddy?' It was the man from the big city. The whole bar went quiet and stood up, I stood up with them. One for all and all that. After a few moments Paddy turned and said;

'Are ye ready?'

We all stood with chests sticking out, ready to put this man in his place and tell him we don't want or need his sort around here telling us what to do. Paddy gave his order and we all duly obliged;

'FECKING RUN.' He shouted.

Everyone ran for the back door, I was looking for Madge. Despite her inability to be able to walk very far, she was at the front of the queue that night. We all stood in the back garden of the bar while Paddy opened the door to the Garda and assured them there was no one drinking after hours in his bar. He even went on to tell them how much he respected the law and wouldn't dream of breaking it. So much for the speech then. I'm just glad Paddy wasn't on our side during the war, he would have let the German's in and made them their dinner.

The Garda seemed satisfied with Paddy's explanation. I think they knew he'd been serving after hours. All they had to do was open the back door, the only other exit in the room. The man may have been from the big city but he was thick as pig shit. This was the same man who some months later was unknowingly harbouring a fugitive. There were wanted pictures plastered around the village of a man who'd committed a crime in Limerick. The man was known to have family in the village, so the likelyhood of him seeking refuge there was probable. The man was given a job cleaning the Garda Barracks and was working there for four months before anyone realised he was the same man in the wanted posters. The big city sergeant said he was so busy looking for the fugitive that he didn't see the resemblance of the man working in his own Barracks.

I'm not saying all the Irish are thick, in England we tell English, Irish and Scot's jokes. Always finishing the joke with the Irishman being the thick one. They do exactly the same, only making us English out to be the thick ones. There was one occasion while I was visiting Ireland I was reading a daily paper. One article attracted my attention, they have a national 'Spot The Ball' competition just like the one we have in England. One week they inadvertibly left the ball in the picture. That in itself was pretty stupid but what I found hilarious was that only two people in the whole country actually spotted the ball correctly.

Paddy closed the door to the Garda and let us all back in the bar. I was looking around for Madge but couldn't see her anywhere, Triona couldn't find her mum either. We checked everywhere, I remember her going into the back garden but didn't recall her coming back in. We went back outside and called out their names, all we could here was giggles coming from the nearby fence. Madge and Bridy had tried to climb the four foot fence to escape the Garda but had both got their knickers caught on barbed wire and couldn't get down. They were laughing like schoolgirls, we eventually got them off the fence.

The only problem we had now was how to get out of the bar without being seen by the Garda, who were still parked across the road waiting. Paddy told us two leave the bar in two's at three-minute intervals. There were about thirty people in the bar. As thick as the sergeant was, surely even he would spot fifteen lots of people filing out of the bar like something out of Noah's Ark at regular intervals, no… the thick shite never suspected a thing. We all met up at the end of the village near the river. There were two cars, so Madge and the rest of the older one's got a lift back while we started the long road home on foot.

Madge was always funny about eating in other people's houses and I could tell she wasn't looking forward to her Christmas dinner. It was a beautiful dinner but she always liked her own cooking. Bridy had told her she was a guest and she must not help prepare the dinner. We all sat around the small table, John said his usual Grace before eating any meal, we all sat with our knives and forks in anticipation. Every time John finished a sentence we would start to eat our food. This was Christmas and this Grace was going on longer than normal. He thanked everyone from Paddy Kelly to the Pope. Our dinner would be cold by the time he'd finished his Grace. It was then I noticed Madge doing something odd, while the rest of them had their eyes shut she was taking food off her plate and putting it under the table. Fuck me, she was doing the 'bank bag' trick, I couldn't believe it. She used to go mad at me for doing that. That day I found a new respect for Madge, it was like finding out your dad was still good at football.

We were leaving Ireland before New Year and our stay was a couple of days shorter than usual. Triona and Patricia said their tearful goodbyes to their mum and dad and Madge thanked them for their hospitality and we headed for the long journey to Dublin to catch our ferry home. The Irish Sea was back to it's usual tempestuous self. The sea gods had abandoned Madge this time, probably due to her bank bag trick while John was saying Grace.

She headed straight for the bar and bought herself a Whiskey and Lemonade, she drank about five of them until she eventually fell asleep with her coat on. The crossing was quite rough, nothing compared to the English Channel but rough enough. It was about three O'clock in the morning and the ferry was quiet, most people were asleep. They would soon to be woken up with the news that the boat was sinking. Madge was convinced we were sinking and was shouting for people to get their life-jackets, everyone started to panic until the Captain came out and reassured everyone all was fine. He gave Madge a good telling off for frightening everyone, I found it quite funny if not a little embarrassing. We nearly made the whole trip without Madge doing something we would talk about for years to come.

Aunty Mavis's new years party was soon upon us and the same old faces were there, except the woman from next door. She'd left the clairvoyant ambulance man. He apparently came home from work one day and she'd gone, run off with another fella… bet he didn't see that one coming.

CHAPTER SEVENTEEN

MOVING ON.

The party went as usual, dad turned up with Shirley. She was becoming a constant companion, she was about ten years younger than dad. He no doubt told her he was a millionaire. It was no surprise when he said he was moving in with her. Shirley had three grown children and a grandson, dad had a ready-made family and once again they would become his priority. It wasn't such a problem for me, I had bigger fish to fry but it upset Donna as she had two beautiful daughters who wouldn't get to see their granddad as much as this new kid on the block.

He even phoned Donna and told her it was his new 'grandson's' second birthday and not to forget his card. That was met with the contempt it deserved, we didn't blame Shirley or the little boy, they didn't know our dad like we did. It was just a case of him, as usual getting his priorities wrong.

In all the years I'd known him he never once was wrong, no matter what the situation, he always 'played the game' as he famously put it.

Triona never saw that side of my dad until we were sat in gran Karalius' house one Saturday afternoon. It was the week after Mavis' New Years party, we were getting gran some bits of shopping when dad walked in, he introduced us to a woman named Elma and said they'd just started going out together. This was one week after he'd announced he was moving in with Shirley. Triona looked at me in amazement, I wasn't one little bit shocked. Elma had recently moved to the area from Somerset after a divorce that left her quite well off, there was his motive. To keep Shirley in the lifestyle he'd promised her he'd have to get the money from somewhere… that's where Elma came in. He even used Elma's car to take Shirley on days out.

His relationship with Shirley only lasted over a year, I think the breaking point with her was when she fell off a ladder while decorating and broke both her wrists. Instead of dad phoning for an ambulance and getting her to the hospital, he picked her up and took her outside then laid her near a cracked pavement, saying she'd tripped over on it so they could claim compensation from the council. He couldn't see anything wrong with that. His attitude was;

'She'd broke her wrists anyway, why not use it to their advantage?'

I often wonder when dad was on his own, in his quieter moments did he ever take any responsibility for what he did. After all he was an intelligent man and it was he who used to coin the phrase 'You can lie to everyone around you but when you put your head on the pillow at night, you can't lie to yourself.'

I've not portrayed dad very well, I don't think he meant half the things he did and I'm sure he loved us in his own way. He just never showed it very much, maybe it is synonymous with his generation or the fact he was a mans man and they don't show their emotions. Or maybe he was just like his dad. Madge once told me about the time she first met my gran Karalius, she was sat in the living room when granddad walked in from work, Madge had put her coat over the armchair. Granddad walked past the coat and stopped, he about turned and picked her coat up then threw it in the garden;

'Coat stand or the garden.' He said calmly.

He was said to be a harsh, stubborn man, gran didn't get on with him at all. Even though his name was Vithau she would call him Frank just to annoy him. On the day of my granddad's funeral gran Karalius was sobbing into a handkerchief, uncle Vin saw this and said;

'Pack it in mam, everyone knew you didn't like him.'

As long as I remember gran Karalius had a handkerchief to her nose. She always took snuff and would hide behind the newspaper thinking no one knew what she was doing, dad would always say to her;

'Why don't you stop shoving that stuff up your nose?'

'You stop throwing all your money on the pissing horses and I'll stop putting shite up me nose… until then keep yer shitty remarks to yerself.' Was her reply.

You never realise your parents had a life before you came along, I was shocked when I heard some of the things dad got up to in his earlier days before I was even a twinkle in his eye. How he sold a fifty-foot iron bridge that wasn't his. He and two of his cronies noticed some demolition work being undertaken at an old bridge in Chester, dad got in touch with some guy from Birmingham and asked him would he be interested in two hundred ton of scrap iron from a bridge his company was dismantling. The guy jumped at the chance and arranged to meet him in Chester. Dad turned up in his best suit and took the guy to the site where the bridge was. He put on a hard hat and walked around the site with the guy. No one thought twice to ask what dad was doing, it just looked like dad was in charge, he even shouted up to one of the lads;

'Finish that off and go and get some dinner and get me my usual will you?' The lad was too high up to question what he was saying. As dad was walking towards one of the cabins to hold a meeting with this poor bastard, dad got a previously arranged call on the Walkie Talkie he'd purchased. It was one of dads mates sat on an embankment near by. Dad told the guy he had some urgent business to take care of at another site but would meet him in a hotel he said he was staying at that night to complete the transaction. He then booked a room under a false name in a top Chester hotel. The guy from Birmingham went to the hotel and asked for Mr King, my dad. They ate and drank and thrashed out a deal. Dad said he'd need a down payment in advance to ensure the guy wouldn't pull out of the deal, this was common practice back then. The guy from Birmingham gave dad a suitcase of money, five thousand pounds and the rest when dad delivered the scrap. Dad gave him a receipt and shouted the desk clerk over and asked him to put the case in the safe until the next day. Everything seemed kosher, the man didn't suspect a thing. He thought he'd just bought a bridge. What he didn't know was the desk clerk was actually one of dad's mates in a suit who took the case full of money straight outside to the car. Dad stayed with the guy for an hour or so and told him he would meet him the following day at the bridge. The man never saw my dad or his money again.

Then there was the time when he and five of his mates pulled up in a pick-up truck in Wigan, donned yellow vests and hard hats and put barriers around the area, then removed 350 paving flags from the street. No one said a word to them, why would they? People just thought it was a gang of workmen getting on with their job.

I went with dad to Bolton Wanderers football ground some years ago, we sat in the car park in his red Vauxhall Viva for about half an hour when a Jaguar pulled along side us, the window of the Jaguar wound down and someone passed dad an envelope through the window and drove off. He opened the envelope and counted out two thousand pounds in cash. I didn't know why he got the money and knew I shouldn't ask. I did ask could I hold it, I'd never seen that sort of money before. As we went to drive away, the car broke down. Dad said we'd have to hitch a lift home and come back for the car the following day. Before we got to the motorway on foot a car stopped and asked us the way to Warrington, dad's eyes lit up. Warrington is the next town to Widnes. He told the Asian guy in the car if he could give us a lift he'd show him, as we'd broke down. The guy, a Doctor as it turned out agreed. I was sat in the back and noticed we were approaching the Warrington exit, dad kept the doctor talking until we arrived in Widnes, just outside grans house. We'd gone past Warrington by three miles.

'If you go back in that direction for about three miles mate, that's Warrington you can't miss it.' He said.

Another time we were driving through Manchester and got lost. We had to ask for directions, before we did dad said that if you ever ask a man for directions, he'd always direct you via pubs. We pulled up and dad asked some guy the way to Trafford Park?

'No problem mate, turn left at the 'White Feather,' carry on for one hundred yards 'til you get to 'The dog and duck' then take a right and it's there, right across from the 'Flying pig' mate.'

Dad was right. Someone stopped and asked me for directions some time ago and subconsciously I too directed them via the local pubs. It must be something only men do. I wonder how women would direct someone? Via hairdressers or bingo halls maybe… I don't know.

Madge used to say men are a strange breed and never grew up, she had a point. Even now when you watch these home made video camera programmes, nine times out of ten it's a grown man who thinks it's a good idea to ride down a steep hill on his son's new skateboard with the inevitable disastrous outcome. It's just not the sort of thing women do at that age… us men are fucking stupid.

I sometimes worry that I myself am carrying on the Karalius male bloodline and am picking up their bad habits. Only last week my son came in from football and he said he was starving, the first words out of my mouth were;

'Starving… starving, you don't know the meaning of the word. There are kids in Africa who…' Fuck, I had to stop myself. I was turning into my dad.

The reason I've spent most of this chapter devoted to my dad is that I was attempting to show a lighter side to him. A more human side. I've failed miserably I know, maybe you just can't find something that wasn't there in the first place. Sorry dad I tried.

There are times in your life when you are shoved into a direction you didn't particularly want to go in. Circumstances dictate to you and you feel you have no choice. Maybe that's what happened to my dad. Nobody wants to be addicted to gambling… it just happens!

That moment in my life was fast approaching. Only it was my right leg and the freak football accident that I had dictating to me. I was seriously thinking about going to Germany with work despite the doctor's warnings. That decision was soon to be made for me.

My time working at Ford's Motors was about to come to an abrupt end. I'd had a lot of time off because of my leg and even though they were sympathetic, they told me they had to let me go. I understood but sympathy wouldn't pay the rent on the flat, I didn't have the luxury to be able to rest. I had three choices, go back and work on the side with dad and risk my health, move back in with Madge and sleep on the settee. Or go and live in Ireland.

I told Triona we would move to Ireland within the next three months. We had just enough money to pay the rent for that long and that would maybe buy me some time. Time to rest and after that find another job so I didn't have to go and live in The Emerald Isle. I told her not to tell anyone of our decision, not until the time was right. I was of course hoping that the time would never have to come.

The next two months I did nothing but rest my leg, I would sit at the front window every market day and watch people coming in and out. I noticed that the 'fresh' pies that were to be sold on a Friday were actually taken in the market on a Thursday morning when the market was closed, nobody would ever know. But they didn't count on my prying eyes from behind the net curtain. I told everyone I knew;

'Don't buy the pies, they're not fresh.'

I thought I was doing a public service when in fact I was turning into an interfering old biddy at the age of twenty-one who had nothing better to do than to nosy from behind the curtains. I realised life in Ireland wouldn't be too different than this, except I would have nowhere to go, nowhere to hide. I voiced my concerns to Triona but she was counting the days until she went home and she told me I could get work over there on building sites, so I wouldn't have time to be bored.

While she was at work I would sit in the pub in the afternoon and arrive home late, I told her I was just having a last hurrah! Looking back I think I was trying to force her hand, she'd decide she'd had enough of me and go back to Ireland on her own. That would've been easy, the decision would have been made for me.

Life's never that easy. As the time was drawing nearer to our move I was becoming more and more apprehensive. I hadn't told anyone I was going yet. Dad wouldn't care either way and I didn't know how Donna would react. It was Madge I was dreading telling, she wasn't over keen on Triona to begin with.

We'd already given four weeks notice to the owner of the flat. There was no turning back. I went to Madge's flat, Donna's car was parked outside. I could kill two birds with one stone. I let myself in and told them I had something to tell them.

Donna hit the roof and said I was stupid, she stormed out of the flat and never spoke to me again before I left. Madge was quiet, I could see she was upset but told me it was my life and had to do what I thought best. I thought the reaction would have been the other way around. I couldn't understand why Donna was so against me moving to Ireland, I'd always supported her in everything she did. I even argued with Madge on her behalf when she married Peter.

Stacey's Christening was the following Sunday, I was one of the Godfather's, with the situation with Donna I thought it would be awkward but it wasn't. The Christening was at St. Johns Protestant church, it was packed with all the family, mainly catholics. If you haven't ever been in a Protestant church with a catholic before, I recommend it, if only for the comedy value. Gran Karalius and aunty Mavis walked in the church and immediately scanned the enemy territory, they shuddered and give themselves the Sign of the Cross. They must have thought god was going to strike them dead on the spot. I could see the rest of the catholics comparing the modern interior to their more traditional style church. One of Peters elderly relatives actually stood at the back near the doorway and said;

'I'll stand here for Stacey's sake, but you know me Peter I'd rather go to a whorehouse than step foot in a 'proddy-dog' church.'

I've been to many Christenings over the years but nothing compared to this one. On one side of the aisle all the family were sat, on the other side were the regular congregation. They were proper 'Bible Bashers' and were singing their praises to the lord, eyes shut and hands waving in the air. We were all looking across in amazement, even I felt embarrassed just for being a protestant, I felt like apologising to all the 'Catlicks' on the congregations behalf. Vicars are like Estate Agents, once you're in their building you're not getting out until they've said what they have to say and sell you what they've got to sell you. This particular vicar was trying to sell us god, even after the actual ceremony of dipping Stacey in the font, he went on and on. I by this time had hold of our Jenna, I was willing her to start crying so I had an excuse to go outside. It was the first and last time I ever contemplated pinching my baby niece on the arm just so she would scream. He stood preaching about how the Lord would save us from our sins and allow us into his Holy kingdom. His congregation hanging on his every word, he was like a religious pop-star;

"HALLELUJAH!" They would shout at the end of every sentence. The Catholics were becoming really freaked out and shuffling uneasily.

Out of the blue a woman dressed in a nightgown ran on the stage screaming;

'Don't listen to my husband… Jesus failed me in my hour of need.' She was dragged off behind the curtains kicking and screaming. The service was thankfully cut shorter than usual. We went to the Columba Hall for the party aftrewards, the Catholics were relishing in the debacle that they'd just witnessed. Trouble was not even the most staunch Protestant could defend that service, I don't think anyone was converted that day, put off maybe but definitely not converted.

I got home from the Christening a little worse for wear, I wet the baby's head alright. When I got in the living room I thought we'd been burgled. All that was in the living room was a couch and the television, Triona had packed everything away ready for the move, it was three weeks away. She didn't come to the Christening, I thought it best due to Donna's mood. Triona informed me that the removal van was coming the following week to take all our things to Ireland.

We sat on boxes for nearly two weeks, I watched the removal van drive away with all my things, I wanted to shout it back and tell Triona I'd changed my mind. But there was another side of me that thought it might work out okay. It was becoming real now, Donna still wouldn't speak to me and Madge was becoming more agitated the closer it got.

The night before the move soon arrived, my mates from Leggies took me out for a farewell drink. I was staying at Madge's flat for one last night. Triona stayed with her sister. We'd arranged to meet at my dad's flat the following morning where Ryan would pick us up and take us to Speke Airport in Liverpool.

I left the pub at ten-thirty, I didn't want to be drunk, I wanted to remember my last night with my mum. Madge and I sat up playing Trivial Pursuit, I could see her eyes were getting tired but she wouldn't go to bed. I felt like a condemned man holding on to every hour. We never spoke about Ireland, we just laughed and talked about times gone by. It was almost three O'clock in the morning, Madge said she had to go to bed. She held my head in her hands and kissed me on the forehead;

'I love you Andrew, I don't think I'll see you again after tomorrow.' This wasn't a guilt trip, I could tell she meant it. I told her not to be stupid and that I'd be over at every opportunity. She wished me a good night and went to bed.

I sat up on my own until daybreak, I heard Madge getting up. She made me a full English breakfast and sat quietly. I looked at the clock, I had to go. I stood up and was choking back the tears, Madge put her head in her hands and started to sob. I put my arms around her and told her I loved her. I got to the bottom of the stairs when she shouted me, she was stood on the top of the landing with tears streaming down her face;

'I'm sorry, I've always loved you.' She said.

'I know mum, I've always known.' I replied before shutting the door behind me.

I scraped the skin off my knuckles when I shut the door, I don't know why I remember that… I just do. I walked over the Golf course to my dads flat, the tears were streaming down my face. I could imagine Madge sat in the flat all alone crying. I felt like I'd abandoned her and couldn't get her words out of my head;

'I'll never see you again.'

Sometimes there's a pain in your stomach you can't get rid of. That morning was one of those times, even now as I sit here writing nearly twenty years on, I can still see her stood at the top of the landing and feel the same pain in my stomach. Tears roll down my cheek as I recall that day in Madge's flat. This is one chapter I was dreading writing. Chapter seventeen… Moving on.

CHAPTER EIGHTEEN

Bringing up… Chickens?

I looked down at the Irish Sea from the plane. The 'fasten your seat belts' sign came on. I looked down at the sea and saw the shadow of the plane on the water, we were about to land at Dublin Airport. Triona was excited and I understood that, I looked at my knuckles and wondered what Madge was doing now, was she still upset?

We arrived in the village, this time there was no reception. This time it wasn't a holiday it was permanent. When we got to the house Triona's mum and dad hugged her and welcomed her back home. I was an after thought, her dad told me to make myself at home. They went to one of their neighbours to show Triona off, I guess it's unusual for someone to actually come back to Ireland. I sat in the chair and looked around, this was my latest 'new' home, it didn't feel that way.

I was shocked when Triona told me she was to start work in a sewing factory in the near by town of Tullamore. She had made inquiries about the job when we were last over in Ireland. I told her she must have been confident that I would decide to come over here to live, given the fact she'd sorted a job out. She looked at me coldly and said;

'Not really, I would have come back anyway.'

I myself had some luck on the job front. JD was building a porch at a house in the village. He knew I'd had some experience in building and asked if I wanted two-weeks work helping him. I jumped at the chance. I had to laugh at the thought of an 'Irish man' and a 'Porch,' it reminded me of a joke I heard back in England.

An English man and an Irish man had been laid off work at a building site. The foreman felt sorry for the Irishman as he had a family and Christmas was approaching. He told the Irishman to go to the shed and get the green paint, he then told him to go to the foreman's house and paint his porch with the green paint and he would pay him one hundred pounds on his return. The Irishman came back after two hours and went to the foreman's office.

'Have you finished?' Asked the foreman.
'Yes.' The Irishman replied.
'Only problem was boss… it wasn't a Porsche… it was a Mercedes!'

I've helped build a couple of porches over the years. I could never understand why people would want one. They cost a few hundred quid to build, they don't add any value to your house and are only ever big enough to house two pairs of muddy shoes and an umbrella. I think they're a statement to the neighbours. 'Look at us, we couldn't afford a conservatory but we've got a porch.'

Calling at a house that has a porch always leaves me with a dilemma. Do I knock on the outside door, or do I open the outside door and enter the porch and knock on the original front door. If I am brave enough to enter the porch, for some reason I will knock on the inside door and run back outside to wait for an answer. I hate porches.

I enjoyed working with JD, he told stories of his time in prison. I told him he should write a book, it would be hilarious.

'I can't spell for shite.' He replied.

I was pleased with the end result and was sure we would get more work when people saw the finished product. That was wishful thinking, it was apparent why most Irish builders were in England, the work in Ireland was scarce. I would help Triona's dad chop wood and helped him picking potatoes, but my day consisted of getting up at about nine am and walking to the village for a newspaper. The Daily Mirror crossword was the highlight of my day. Triona and her mum and dad were out at work all day, I'd sit and watch the television and do the crossword then prepare the tea for when the workers came home. I'd turned into an Irish housewife.

The football season had started and I began light training, I only played two games and it was evident my leg had put an end to my playing days. That depressed me even further, the one thing I used to be good at had been cruelly taken away from me. I wasn't even good enough to get in a village team in the middle of the Irish countryside.

The honeymoon period was over, the realisation that this wasn't a holiday was beginning to dawn on me. Triona and I were drifting apart, we were becoming more like brother and sister. I was still sleeping in the spare room and our sex life was none existent.

One morning I went into the chicken coup to collect the mornings fresh eggs. To my surprise there were twelve little yellow fluffy chicks. I'd never seen baby chicks before, I ran back into the house and told John. He told me he would keep them until they were fully grown, then he would sell them, if they survived the foxes and herons, that is. I made it my full time job to protect these chicks. I made a corrugated iron coup in the back garden and put wire meshing over the top so the herons couldn't get in. At first the mother hen wouldn't let me near her or the chicks, but I still went back twice daily to leave them food and water. The mother must have got used to me, after a while she would let me in the coup and pick the chicks up, I was a surrogate father to twelve baby chicks and a husband to a hen. It sounds ridiculous but those chicks gave me something to get up for in the morning, first thing I would do is to go and check how they were and leave them some food and water. It was due to the chicks that I saw a UFO, I was lay in bed when I heard a noise coming from the back yard. I thought it was a fox. I jumped up and grabbed the poker from the fireplace and crept outside, I couldn't see anything. The chicken coup seemed fine. As I turned to go back into the house I noticed a bright light in the sky, it was like an orange light hovering high above the house. Was it a UFO? Well I couldn't identify it, it was flying and it was definitely an object… so I guess it was. I watched it for about five minutes until it disappeared into the distance. I honestly don't know what I saw that night but it sent a chill down my spine. Like most things paranormal, I like to keep an open mind. I do think it would be naïve, arrogant even to think that in the vast universe we are the only living beings. I just wished if I had seen aliens that night they would have abducted me and took me back to England. It's not like anyone would have noticed, except maybe the chicks.

The nights were the worst, we all would just sit in the living room watching Irish television until about nine O'clock, then they would all go to bed ready for work the next morning. The television would stop transmitting at eleven thirty. It was like living in the past.

I would look forward to the letters from home, Madge wrote once a week and dad would send me some money over every couple of weeks or so. The money came in handy, I'd wait for the postman and run to the mail and check was there any letters for me. Madge would tell me how everything was going with Stacey and Jenna and told me the doctors had put her on more tablets. Dad would sent me twenty-pounds and a note saying 'From dad.' I would go to the village and change the twenty-pound note into an Irish twenty-Punt note. Then I would sit in the bar and get drunk until my money ran out.

It was on one such occasion that spelled the beginning of the end of my time in Ireland. It was Triona's dad's birthday the following week and Patricia and Ryan sent him a card from England with a twenty-pound note in it. The card never arrived, which wasn't unusual. My letters sometimes didn't arrive. He accused me of opening his birthday card and taking the money out.

'I know ye changed a twenty in the post office, I was told.' He shouted.

I told him dad sent me some money over and even showed him the letter it came in. I don't think he believed me. Our relationship didn't get any better when I borrowed his bike to go to the village. It was a very old bike that belonged to his father. On the next occasion dad sent me some money, I jumped on the old bike and went to the village. I again changed the money and headed for the bar. I was in there for about four hours and was pissed as a newt. I remember walking outside and staggering on the bike, I started to pedal but just went around in a circle until I landed flat on my face. I eventually got going in the right direction. I was half way up the lane when I felt myself going to the left. I couldn't stop myself, I went through the bushes and landed in the ditch. The front wheel on the bike was buckled. I staggered to my feet and left the bike in the ditch, someone picked me up and dropped me at the house.

I awoke the next day to here John shouting, I wondered what was the matter with him. I heard the word bicycle mentioned. I lay on the bed and the previous day slowly started coming back to me;

'Fuck... the bike, where did I leave it?' I said to myself.

I racked my brain, but I was that pissed I just couldn't remember. I looked down at my hand and it was muddy... the ditch, it was all coming back to me. I decided to wait for John to go out and I would go and get his bike out of the ditch, no harm done. When I got to the ditch the bike had gone, I was pretty sure this was were I left it. The gap in the hedges where I'd crashed was evident and there were tyre tracks in the mud.

The bike was never found and John never spoke to me again. I couldn't blame him, he was a simple man with simple values. I'd come here, lived in his home, ate his food and lost his dads bike.

Things came to a head one Sunday evening, I was sat watching the television at around ten-thirty in the evening on my own when a programme came on about polluted rivers. Normally I wouldn't watch a programme like this but it was the best of a bad lot. It showed the top ten polluted rivers in the UK. Number three was the river Mersey, the presenter was taking samples from the banks of the Mersey and in the background was the Widnes-Runcorn Bridge. I noticed a red and white bus going over the bridge, it was a Widnes bus. I probably knew someone on that bus. My mind was made up, I decided it was time to go home.

The next day I waited for everyone to go to work and hitched a lift into Tullamore, I booked a one way ticket to Holyhead. I never told Triona, I would just go. The earliest ticket I could get was the following Wednesday, I had two days left in Ireland and was counting the hours.

Wednesday morning arrived and I was booked on the four-thirty ferry from Dublin, I had to move fast. As Triona walked out of the house to go to work I shouted her back;

'What's wrong?' She asked.

'Nothing, I just want to say see you later.' I replied.

I then kissed her on the cheek and watched her walk down the lane for the last time, she stopped half way down the lane and looked back at me, she looked sad. I think she knew I was leaving. She put up her hand, turned and carried on walking.

I went into the back garden to say goodbye to the chickens, I left them their food and water, got my bags and again hitched a lift into Tullamore. I got the train into Dublin. My ferry wasn't for another two hours, so I did what I did best… found a bar and had a drink.

I never saw Triona again, we spoke on the phone. I told her she could keep the furniture. Ryan brought the rest of my things home when he went to Ireland the following month. I heard some months later that she was engaged to be married to a lad from the factory she worked in, I wondered was she seeing him while I was in Ireland? It didn't matter, the young man died of a heart-attack. Triona was devastated I believe. I genuinely felt sorry for her when I heard the news, although I didn't love her or she me, I wished her no harm and every happiness for the future.

When I recall my first few visits to Ireland I see a light green colour surrounding the memory. When I recall the time I went to live there I see dark black green with heavy clouds over head. With a little bit of yellow… my chickens.

I met two Australian guys in the bar and we had a few drinks. They were going to the airport to go home. I don't know how people sleep in

Australia, they have the most deadliest animals on the planet. I still check the ceiling for the common house spider before I go to sleep at night. Not because I'm scared of them but they reckon in every humans lifetime we eat on average of ten spiders each, that's bad enough but imagine waking up with a deadly spider on your face… no, I could never go to Australia.

I stood at the back deck on the ferry to Anglesey that day, watching the grand city of Dublin become smaller and smaller with each passing minute. I wasn't sad to see the back of it and swore I'd never go back to Ireland again. Don't get me wrong, I never saw enough of the country to be able to pass judgement and I'm sure it's a beautiful country but I'd seen enough of the Emerald Isle and I think it had seen enough of me.

I didn't tell anyone I was coming home, I couldn't wait to see Madge again and the surprise on her face when she seen me. I'd only been away for just over two months but it seemed a lot longer.

I arrived in Anglesey at four-thirty in the morning. I then had to get a train to Crewe. From there I would have to wait four hours for a train to take me to Liverpool. I just wanted to get home so I phoned my dad and asked could he pick me up from Crewe Station. He arrived one hour later and nearly hugged me when he saw me, then he remembered who he was and gave me a manly handshake instead.

I recall driving along the motorway and seeing the Runcorn-Widnes Bridge in the distance, my stomach turned. Then the smell hit me, the smell of the Grannox Abattoir located in West Bank on the river Mersey. It's a smell of dead animals and a smell I and every other Widnesian had complained about all of our lives. This time was different. I wound down the window and took a deep breath. 'Home,' I thought to myself.

It was eight O'clock in the morning, dad asked if I wanted to go to a greasy spoon for some breakfast. I had a full English, the girl behind the counter asked would I like Ulster fry on my breakfast. Ulster fry is an Irish alternative to bacon. I gave an ironic laugh and said;

'No thanks… bacon's fine.'

For the first time my dad treated me like a man that morning in the greasy spoon on the West Bank Dock Estate. It wasn't anything he said or done in particular. He just seemed different. He dropped me off at Madge's flat, I stood for a minute before I knocked on the door. I still had a key but that would have killed the effect, the element of surprise. I finally knocked on the door, I heard her coming down the stairs;

'OK, give me a minute.' She shouted.

She opened the door and stared at me, I don't think she knew what to say. I broke the silence;

'I'm home mum… for good.'

She started to cry and threw her arms around me. I felt like a hero returning from war, I carried my bags up the stairs. Madge told me she was making me a proper full English breakfast;

'None of that Irish shit you've been eating.' She said.

I didn't have the heart to tell her that dad had just bought me a breakfast and I was stuffed, I was forcing the food down me, I didn't even have any bank bags!

I didn't get any sleep on the ferry and was tired, Madge told me to go and have a lie down in her bed. I awoke just after dinner and heard voices coming from the living room. Madge had ran to a neighbours house and phoned Donna to tell her I was home. I walked in the living room and Donna simply said;

'Do you want to come and see the girls?'

We all got ready and went to Donna's house, it had only been a couple of months but my nieces had got so big. I was glad to be home and I know this sounds awful but the only thought I gave to Ireland was 'were the chickens alright?' I never really gave a second thought to Triona and she never tried to get in touch with me for over a week.

She eventually rang Donna and asked me to phone her later that night. I was getting my explanation ready, I thought she'd be furious with me but she wasn't. It confirmed what I already thought, she didn't want me back there as much as I didn't want to be there. She actually apologised to me for dragging me over to Ireland. I told her it was my fault, it all ended quite amicably. Over two years of our life wasted, I learnt a valuable lesson though. I swore I would never do anything I didn't want to do again.

Madge and I rekindled our love affair with Trivial Pursuit and I rekindled my love affair with Leggies and the demon drink.

I started to work with dad again and was still sleeping on Madge's settee. I'd had my time of playing an adult and was quite happy to cling on to Madge's apron strings once again. Madge's health was deteriorating, we never knew how bad it was because she did have a tendency to exaggerate and let us know how many new tablets the doctor had given her. She was only fifty-six but acted a lot older. I think it's a thing women do when they get to a certain age, they like to tell complete strangers how old they are, just so the stranger will tell them they look ten years younger and they like to tell people how ill they are. This may not be the case with all women but it's certainly the case with any woman I've ever known. Take gran Karalius for example, she would tell people she was ninety-six when in fact she was only eighty-five, so people would tell her she didn't look her age. Before any women reading this book throws it in the fire because I'm generalising… WAIT! Men are worse, men tell everyone they're younger than they really are and find it appropriate to put on a football kit at the age of fifty-two and try to compete with boys half their age, just to regain their youth.

It became apparent in April of 1991 that Madge was not exaggerating her ailments. I was sat in Leggie's pub on a Saturday afternoon when one of Madge's neighbours ran in looking for me;

'It's your mam, she's been taken to Whiston Hospital in an ambulance.' I downed my pint, never one to let a good beer go to waste and phoned Donna. She picked me up and went straight to the hospital. Madge had horrific pains in her stomach and was kept in hospital for tests.

The specialist called Donna and I to the hospital two days later and gave us the news nobody wants to hear about one of their parents. The news that would change my life forever.

CHAPTER NINETEEN

FOR THE GOOD TIMES.

It's only now occurred to me as I near the end of this story. I had the pleasure of being part of Madge's life for twenty-one years. What happened in her life in the thirty-five years previous to me being born? What where her aspirations? Her dreams. I know all about dad in his younger days but nothing about Madge. She never spoke much about her life as a young woman. There was only one place I could get any such information… aunty Bella.

Although I live just around the corner from her I don't see her as much as I should. She reminds me too much of Madge, it brings back all the memories but she is the one person remaining who can tell me what I need to know.

I'd not seen Bella for over six-months, she was older than Madge and was approaching her eightieth birthday. We sat for hours talking about their younger days, stories nobody wants to hear any more, except for me. I sat and listened and wrote notes in my book. Notes I will relay in this penultimate chapter.

I listened to Bella's stories, how she and Madge met dad and Archie at St Marie's dance hall;

'We were stunners back then you know.' I could see that although she was looking at me, she was seeing a time long gone. A happy time. Tears came to her eyes, she still missed Madge very much. I told her I was sorry for bringing it all back up and upsetting her but she assured me she wanted to carry on.

Bella told me how Madge nearly joined Art School when she was nineteen but gran and granddad couldn't afford the fees to send her to

London. Just as well, she would never have met dad and I wouldn't be sitting here writing about her but maybe she would have had a better life. Bellas' tears turned to laughter when she said that her and Madge were sat in a café when they were in their thirties. Two young lads came up to them and asked would they complete a survey they were doing for college. They asked Madge and Bella what they enjoyed doing in their spare time? Bella replied 'Sex… we love sex.' The young boys went a pale colour and made a quick exit;

'We terrified those young lads, you couldn't see their arses for dust.' Bella recalled with howls of laughter. Then her laughter turned to a more sombre mood;

'We had some great times, your mam and me. The day she died, a part of me went with her.' She said staring at Madge's picture on the old sideboard that used to belong to gran Holland.

That brought me on to my next question, could I borrow some pictures of Madge. I've never been one for keeping pictures and have noticed that people always seem to put pictures up of people after they've died. I looked around Bella's house and most of the pictures on her wall were of family members who'd long gone. I'm not saying there's anything wrong with it, it's probably her way of coping. But I like to keep all my pictures in my head, that way I can look at them any time I want. Old photographs do fascinate me though. What was going through their mind the minute that camera shot a moment in time, where were they going after that photo was taken?

I said goodbye to aunty Bella and thanked her. She told me I should come around more often to see her. I told her that I would but I knew I'd always find an excuse not to go back, there's no point in trying to hold on to the past, it's gone and you can never get it back. I didn't feel sorry for Bella, she has a big family and the house is always busy. She wouldn't miss me going around raking up the past.

My wife used to work in a home for the elderly. I would occasionally go and sit in the lounge to wait for her to finish her shift. I would look around at all these old people staring into space or at a blank television screen. Imagine the stories they had to tell, if only someone would listen. Just to take half an hour out of our busy schedule and lend them an ear, imagine the difference that could make to their day. I think care homes should employ people just to do that… listen. The carers and nurses do a great job and do sit with the old people but they have a job to do. It's a job

I could do but then I'm a story-teller and could listen to people's stories all day long.

Donna and I were told that the Specialist at Whiston Hospital wanted to see us. We knew that wasn't a good sign, we never spoke a word on the way to the hospital that day. The clouds were black and the rain was pouring down, it was a horrible day but was about to get a lot worse.

The specialist told us that Madge had lung cancer, which had spread. Donna begged her not to tell Madge about the cancer, that's how gran Holland died and was Madge's phobia. She told Donna she had to tell her. I asked was it terminal, she looked at me and coldly said 'yes.' I know she deals with this every day of her working life but surely she could have been a little more sensitive.

'How long?' Donna asked.

'Weeks... months. Three months tops.' She replied.

Just like in a Hitchcock movie I could feel the office walls closing in on me, my chest started to tighten. I looked at Donna for reassurance, waiting for her to say something, anything but she just sat there in shock. I needed fresh air. I walked out of the office and started walking down the long corridor. My walk turned into a run, I needed to get outside. The exit doors seemed miles away, I was pushing people out of the way to get to them. I sat outside on a bench, two girls walked past me laughing and joking with each other. Buses went past and a young couple came out holding a small baby. The world was still going about its business as if nothing had happened, I've just been told my mum was going to die and the world still dared to go on.

I had to compose myself before I went back in to see Madge. How could I look at her? What would I say? She was sat up in the bed talking to Donna, she didn't even look ill. The doctor had already told Madge about the cancer, they didn't tell her it was terminal. They said they were going to give her chemotherapy. Madge said she was fine and she would fight the cancer. I could tell she was scared and that's what hurt me the most, I wished I could tell her I would sleep under the tree outside so she wasn't alone at night like she said to me all those years ago.

I've never felt pain quite like the pain I felt that day. My stomach was hurting. Donna dropped me off at Madge's flat, I immediately went to Leggies to get pissed. It wouldn't beat the cancer but at least I would forget for a short time.

Donna had gone to the council and arranged for Madge to get a ground floor flat so she didn't have to climb the stairs when she got out of hospital, we didn't want her final months to end in hospital. The flat was around the corner from Donna's house and was ideal.

Madge started chemotherapy the following day, I never went to see her for two days. People criticised me for that but I couldn't watch my mum dying. Instead I got pissed and wallowed in my own self-pity. Donna was to pick Madge up the following Sunday and take her to see her new flat and have some lunch, she'd arranged to pick me up on the way. She told me that Madge looked quite poorly due to the treatment and I was not to be shocked. I waited in the car, we had the girls with us. They were too young to understand what was going on. What happened next I will never forget for the rest of my life. I saw Donna coming out of the hospital pushing an old woman in a wheelchair. I wondered what she was doing? Where was Madge? As they drew closer I could see the old lady was Madge. My mum had aged twenty-years in three days, I could see the tears in Donna's eyes. I got out of the car and put Madge in the back with the girls, she was quiet but when she did speak her words were slurred and she had white stuff on her lips. We stopped at the Town Hall while Donna went to collect the keys for the flat. Madge asked me if she was talking funny, I choked back the tears and assured her it was the medicine she was on.

We arrived at the flat and took Madge in to have a look around she said she loved the flat and then told us;

'I'll never get to live here.' Before a tear ran down her cheek.

We told her not to be stupid and we meant it, we thought she would come out of hospital and spend her remaining days in her new home. Madge was right, she never got to live there. We visited Madge every night after that. I would always go to the pub afterwards and get paralytic. It was my way of coping, although I didn't really need an excuse to get drunk back then.

On one such night I fell out of the pub and went to Madge's flat to sleep it off. I awoke the next day around dinner-time. Still feeling rough from the night before I stumbled to the bathroom. I noticed something had been posted through the door, it was a letter telling me to phone the police immediately. I wondered what the fuck I'd done the night before. I ran over to Leggies and rang the number, I was put through to the desk sergeant. He told me to ring my brother-in-law Peter, it was urgent. I then rang Peter;

'I've been knocking at the flat, where have you been?' He asked.

'You better get to the hospital, your mum's dying.' He went on.

Madge

I told him I knew Madge was dying and what was the urgency. His voice softened as he delivered the dreaded news;

'Andy… she's dying now mate.'

I dropped the phone and asked one of the lads in the pub to run me to the hospital. I ran to the ward but Madge wasn't there, her bed was empty. I thought I was too late. The nurse recognised and showed me to another room, a side ward;

'Your mum's in there.' She said sympathetically.

I put my hand on the door handle and looked back at the nurse, she smiled and put her head down before walking away. I walked in the room and there she was. My mum lay in a bed with tubes and wires coming out of her. The very thing she never wanted. Everyone looked at me. Fiona, Bella, Pat and Donna were all sat around the bed. Donna was holding Madge's hand, I got a chair and sat at the other side of the bed and held her other hand. We took turns in sitting with Madge;

'It's what she would have wanted, all her family here.' Fiona said with a sympathetic smile.

'Like fuck she would.' I thought to myself. But this was not the time or the place to voice any such opinions. I looked down at Madge, her breathing was erratic. Every breath seemed to last for an eternity. I never had an opinion on Euthanasia before but I would definitely of put Madge out of her misery if I could. It amazes me how in a civilised society we still allow our loved ones to suffer. If it was our favourite pet we could take it to the Vets and have it put to sleep to save any unnecessary suffering.

Bella, Fiona and I went to get a cup of tea and sat in the day room. Bella was telling stories from when Madge worked at the Labour Club. There was a barmaid called Joan Roderick, Madge and her never got on. Bella told how Madge would play tricks on Joan and make her life difficult. The conversation was innocuous and we soon moved onto another subject. Bella's anecdotes lightened the mood. We finished our tea and went back into the side ward. It was then a strange thing happened, Madge suddenly awoke from her coma and asked for a fag. Donna was ecstatic and thought it was a miracle, I was less convinced. I'd heard of people taking their last breaths before. Fiona opened her purse to get out her handkerchief and dropped some money on the floor;

'Bloody hell, look at the moths flying out of that purse.' Madge joked.

We all laughed, Madge looked at Donna then at me and smiled. She only smoked half of her cigarette and layback down saying she was tired. Before she shut her eyes she looked over at aunty Bella and said;

'Tell Joan Roderick I'm sorry.'

How did she know we were talking about Joan only hours before in a room at the other end of the corridor? Was she there? Had her spirit already left her dying body? We'll never know, maybe it was just a coincidence.

Donna and I stayed the night, she had to go home early the next morning for a couple of hours to see to the girls. I sat singing *'A Bunch Of Thyme'* to Madge, she responded and tried to sing it with me. My heart was breaking, I considered putting a pillow over her face and put her out of her misery but that wouldn't have been fair on Donna.

Madge lingered for another day but was becoming weaker with each passing hour. I asked the nurse could we get a vicar to give her the last rites, she informed me that there was a priest in the chapel but no vicar. It didn't matter to me who did it, worrying about religion was the furthest thing from my mind. I just thought it was something we should do. Brian had come to see Madge and was in the room, he made a statement that shocked me;

'A priest is okay, your mum was a Catholic anyway.'

I didn't believe him, Madge always lived her life as a Protestant. Fiona confirmed Brian's bombshell. She changed her religion when she married dad so they could get married in St Marie's a Catholic church, Donna was also christened there… as a Catholic. It brought shame to Madge's family and they never spoke of it.

'Am I a catholic?' I asked.

'No, you're probably the only Karalius in the world that isn't.' He replied.

Small wonder dads' family treated me differently. I was an impostor, I always felt different but I thought maybe I was adopted, that's what Donna always told me as a kid. It turns out that because Donna went to a protestant school, St Marie's would not christen me in their church, so I was christened in St Paul's Protestant Church.

The priest came and gave Madge the last rites. I just wanted gran Holland to come and take her, she'd suffered enough. The hours passed and her breathing was less and less, every time she'd take a breath we thought it was her last. She'd breath and then there was a pause for a few seconds, then it started all over again. I looked down at her fingers, they were turning a blue colour. I looked over to Bella and she nodded as if to say, 'not long now.' It was the first time I'd ever seen anyone literally dying, I clutched her hand. Donna was speaking to her the whole time, then finally at twenty-two minutes past twelve in the afternoon Madge let out one big breath. That was her last breath, Donna ran to Peter, she was hysterical. Peter even had a tear in his eye. I just put her lifeless hand to my face, I was glad she wasn't suffering anymore but was devastated that I'd just lost the most important person in my life… my mum, my best friend and the place I called home. I looked around, Fiona, Bella and Pat were hugging each other. Where were my soldiers and my green medicine when I needed them most. Then I realised Madge was the green medicine, the soldiers and everything that was safe in my life. She'd gone and I had no-one to hug.

I now knew exactly how she felt that night when she heard the news that gran Holland had died.

The nurses came and asked us to leave the room for a while. I noticed one of them go over to the window and open it. I didn't know why, I learnt some time later that when somebody dies they open the window to release their spirit.

I was numb, I phoned dad and told him the news;

'Jesus Christ.' Was all he said, despite everything I think he was genuinely upset?

He came up to the hospital within the hour. We were let back into the room. The nurses had cleaned Madge up, she lay on the bed and looked like she was asleep. No more pain no more suffering. I bent over her body and kissed her on the forehead and said;

'Goodnight god bless mum.'

Dad had been in to pay his last respects before me. He'd left a Rose on her pillow with a small card that simply read;

'For the good times.'

'You'll never miss your mothers love, until she's dead and gone.' How right they were.

Marjorie Mary Holland, died June 21st 1991 at Whiston Hospital. An unspectacular person, except to me, she was my mum. Though to most people she was simply known as… Madge!

THE FINAL CHAPTER
Full Circle.

When I first sat down to write this story I couldn't have imagined the memories and emotions it brought back. I've laughed and cried whilst recalling some of the events from my past. I hope it relays the bond Madge and I had, because her love was unconditional. I look back now and think she was one of life's victims. I wonder what her life would have been like if she never met my dad… I wonder?

I had one last thing to do before I could file these memoirs away under 'The Past.' I decided to take one last trip to Sinclair Avenue, the place I hold fondest in my heart. To put some closure on the whole thing.

I jumped in my silver Vauxhall Frontera and drove the short distance to Sinclair. I parked in front of what was once Sarah's house and had a look around. Although it's not far from where I live now, I've not been there for over twenty years. The half moon was now a children's playground with swings and seating. It looked smaller than ever. The old tree that we used as a goalpost was now just a stump, number 26 had new upvc windows and had been brought up to date.

I didn't feel much emotion, I thought I would but this wasn't how I remembered the old house, like everything else… it had moved on.

I wound down my window to get some air into the car. It was a boiling hot day and the road had been newly tarmacked. As I raised my head I thought I saw the half moon field as it was back then and through the heat rising from the tarmac, I swear I saw a young boy stood on the field. He had mousy blond hair with a cow's lick in the middle of his fringe, he wore a Norwich City football top and a pair of Bolton Wanderers shorts. He seemed to recognise me and waved in my direction, I just smiled. I took one last look at the old house. Then back at the young boy, I put my hand up to him and said 'bye' for one last time and drove away.

The End.

Still to come…

Distorted Image.
Life After Madge.

It was my first night in Walton prison, Liverpool. One of the toughest prisons in the country. I was terrified, the cell door slammed shut behind me. It was one of the lowest points in my life. I wondered how I'd ended up here, how had I stooped so low… But that's another story?